Andrew Riemer is a Sydney-b... was born in Budapest in 19... to Sydney, where he has live... universities of Sydney and L....... ... ... the Department of English at the University of Sydney for many years. He is the author of several books on Shakespeare and a regular contributor of book reviews to the *Sydney Morning Herald* and other publications. He is married with two sons.

INSIDE
Outside

LIFE BETWEEN TWO WORLDS

Andrew Riemer

Angus&Robertson
An imprint of HarperCollins*Publishers*

CollinsAngus&Robertson Publishers'
creative writing programme is
assisted by the Australia Council,
the federal government's arts
advisory and support organisation.

AN ANGUS & ROBERTSON BOOK
An imprint of HarperCollinsPublishers

First published in Australia in 1992
Reprinted in 1992 twice
CollinsAngus&Robertson Publishers Pty Limited (ACN 009 913 517)
A division of HarperCollinsPublishers (Australia) Pty Limited
25 Ryde Road, Pymble NSW 2073, Australia

HarperCollinsPublishers (New Zealand) Limited
31 View Road, Glenfield, Auckland 10, New Zealand

HarperCollinsPublishers Limited
77–85 Fulham Palace Road, London W6 8JB, United Kingdom

National Library of Australia
Cataloguing-in-Publication data:

Riemer, A.P. (Andrew P.)
   Inside outside : life between two worlds
   ISBN 0 207 17398 2

   1. Riemer, A.P. (Andrew). 2. Critics—Australia—Biography
   3. English literature—Early modern—History and criticism
   4. College teachers—Australia—Biography.
   I. Title (Series Imprint lives)

820.9003

Cover photograph of the author with Jim Carlton, Bill Blinco,
Suzanne MacAlister and Maggie Blinco.
Typeset in Australia by Midland Typesetters
Printed in Australia by Griffin Paperbacks, Adelaide

5 4 3
95 94 93 92

To
Nina, Tom and Nick
for each equally

If we shadows have offended . . .

PREFACE

This is not an autobiography, but it is a book about the past and the present, generated by deeply personal memories and by the changes I have observed both within myself and in Australian society in the years since the end of the Second World War. It is a book, moreover, with several origins. One occurred on the day in 1947 when I arrived with my parents in Sydney. We were among the first of those waves of postwar European migrants who were to influence the nature of Australian society in various and at times unexpected ways.

Another occasion was almost exactly thirty years later, after my father's sudden death. I realised then that with him, and with my mother who had died three years earlier, many aspects of a family history, a mythology and a way of life had vanished beyond recovery. No-one remained to answer questions about the past or to untangle the complicated relationships of people who had died, often in terrible circumstances, more than thirty years before. I began jotting down vague and discontinuous memories partly for myself, but chiefly so that my sons might have some access to a strange and alien world—which was nevertheless a part of their heritage—before age and the inevitable fading of memory caused more and more of it to disappear.

Those jottings, disjointed fragments of a remembrance of things past, stayed in a drawer of my desk for some years. They were brought to life, and given an entirely unexpected context, by the immediate circumstances that prompted me to write this book: the events of five days that were to prove crucial to my understanding of something that had become a continuing preoccupation. In 1990, a few days before Christmas, I returned to Budapest for the first time since I left it in 1946. The experience of those days in the city where I was born in 1936, the only child of entirely ordinary and unremarkable people who were to become victims of the great upheavals of the thirties and forties, helped to clarify the puzzles of personal and national identity that had governed and shaped much of my thinking about Australian culture, literature and society during the previous twenty years.

As I began to reassemble memories of a half-forgotten past in a city which was simultaneously familiar and entirely alien, I realised that such an act involved more than a private quest for a lost world. I came to understand that my present self was intimately tied to the influence which that place and that society had exerted on me, even though I had grown up among 'Old' Australians, people whose language, customs and social forms I had adopted so thoroughly that I felt alien and out-of-place in Hungary, that landlocked European country which I should have been able to call 'home'. I also realised, as I wandered through the grimy streets, that my private journey of rediscovery and ghost-laying had implications for an understanding of Australian society at the end of a troubled century, a time when the seeds sown by the postwar government's policies of mass-migration were bearing fruit in a manner that the people who had shaped those policies may not have anticipated. This book is the result of that realisation.

Andrew Riemer
SYDNEY, JUNE 1991

OUTSIDE

THE
CUSTOMS
OF THE COUNTRY

When I arrived in Australia in 1947, a few days before my eleventh birthday, the question of multiculturalism had not yet arisen. Everyone assumed that it was the newcomer's duty to fit in, to learn the language, to adopt the customs of the country. Whatever cultural heritage you had brought with you had to be discarded; the past was irrelevant to the new life you were about to forge. With ominous symbolism, the only items from my parents' luggage to be seized by His Majesty's Customs were half a dozen or so decorated wooden platters, garish examples of Hungarian folk art. Now, almost half a century later, the wheel has turned. The dream of a multicultural Australia, a heady brew of contrasted but harmonious cultural strands, has left those of us who listened to our mentors, and tried to assimilate, in some perplexity and confusion.

I have now spent more than three-quarters of my life in this country. My passport tells me that I am an Australian. This is the only society where I feel relatively at ease, safe and comfortable. I depend on it not merely for a livelihood and occupation, but, much more importantly, for the essential and life-sustaining structures of family and friendships. Whenever I am away from Australia, my thoughts turn towards home. Yet I cannot claim to belong here fully. There is a state of mind beyond fondness, or even love, for a country, beyond familiarity or the knowledge that you have carved out a life for yourself in these surroundings. That state of mind is indefinable. To say that it is a lack or a vacancy is an approximation approaching the truth, yet not quite touching it. Nor is it a matter of substitutions: I yearn for Europe, but it is a Europe that no longer exists, and may never have existed. The closest I can get to a description of this condition, dilemma, perplexity, or whatever term may be put upon it, is to say that it is an existence between two worlds: one familiar, substantial, often humdrum and commonplace; the other a country of the mind, fashioned from powerful longings and fantasies. Such longings and fantasies are the products of a complicated network where experience and inheritance intersect.

Perhaps I am merely describing the human condition. I have come to learn that this sense of displacement, of not belonging, even of having been uprooted, is shared by many people whose lives have not been so obviously displaced or uprooted as mine. And yet, as every migrant knows, being obliged to start again, to find that you must remake your life, brings that predicament into sharper focus than might be the case otherwise. To look back at the slow unfolding which began for me on a hot February morning in 1947 is to raise many ghosts, most of which would have been better left undisturbed. It also runs the risk of self-pity and a yearning after the might-have-been. At worst it may seem mere self-indulgence. But the process of learning about and assimilating into an adopted society may, if viewed without rancour or passion, reveal something essential about that society, its values and its problems, which are often seen with greater clarity by the newcomer. Reconstructing that vision many years after the fact entails an alteration of perspective. I am able to look at the past only from the vantage point of my present self. Yet the memory retains enough of those initial impressions, and the present self bears sufficient scars from the past, to make it possible to capture with some accuracy and truth the predicament of those of us who were received by a not entirely welcoming Australia in the years immediately following the war in Europe.

It is only too easy, from the perspective of the much more cosmopolitan society of contemporary Australia, to scoff at the smugly bigoted attitudes of that time. Australia of the immediate postwar years was a narrow, inward-looking society, convinced of its absolute superiority, contemptuous of anything foreign or out of the ordinary. Wherever you went in that low and sunbaked collection of villages called Sydney, you were shown the living and visible proof of that superiority. An incident recorded by Glenda Adams in *Longleg* is echoed by my own experience: the AWA tower, which in those days dominated the city's skyline, was hailed as an astonishing example of engineering and architectural skill. The Harbour Bridge was, of course, the longest single arch suspension bridge in the world. And there were other marvels—the world's longest stretch of straight railway-track; the Burrinjuck dam, unique in the world, or was it in the Southern Hemisphere? 'Isn't this the most wonderful country on earth?' people in the streets would say to you, without a hint of self-consciousness or irony. In some ways they were justified; though, in retrospect, it strikes me as entirely characteristic that these litanies rarely if ever included natural marvels. Many years were to pass before we became aware that there were, indeed, wonders to behold, though not of the man-made sort.

In this cultural and moral climate, my parents and I embarked on the task of assimilating. For some of us the task was easier than for others. Naturally I, as an eleven-year-old, experienced less difficulty than my middle-aged parents. They, in turn, came closer to being absorbed into Australian society than many of their contemporaries, largely because circumstances forced us to live away from those Central European enclaves which were already in existence by the early fifties. But the attempt was ultimately futile—though its futility did not come home to us for very many years. Intrinsically, full assimilation is impossible. At the

3

simplest level, there is nothing you can do about your physical features, no matter how many unconscious fantasies you might entertain about becoming truly Australian. Being Australian, then as now, meant possessing the physical characteristics of people whose forbears came from the British Isles. I became aware of that truth with particular poignancy when I returned to Budapest, the city of my birth, after an absence of more than forty years. My first reaction as I got out of the train and began walking along a noisy, crowded platform—a scene that conjured up the look, indeed the smell of the Balkans—was amazement at seeing all those funny little people milling around me. It took more than a moment's reflection to realise, with a mixture of shame and distress, that I am one of those funny little people.

There are, naturally enough, deeper and much more significant reasons why any naive attempt at becoming absorbed by an alien society must prove futile. I am no physiologist. I do not know to what extent cultural characteristics, in addition to the physical, are encoded in one's genes. But it is evident—and should have been evident to all of us in that dreamtime of the late forties and early fifties— that you cannot discard the complex, contradictory but fundamental reticulation of manners, ethical priorities and social conventions, in short the individual's cast of mind, which are the outward and visible signs of an inner cultural reality. Trying to deny or to reject them makes you run the risk of becoming a simulacrum, a pretence, or, in the worst instance, a parody. You may, it is true, become proficient in the language. It is easy enough to realise that it is not polite to sprinkle salt over your food, whereas placing it in a little heap on the side of the plate (anathema to Central European notions of good table manners) is entirely acceptable. You notice soon enough that forks should be held with the tines pointing downwards, and that you must spoon your soup away from, rather than towards, your person. But you cannot change the intimate, deeply-ingrained, essentially mysterious core of the personality which seems to be

4

implanted very early in life—perhaps stamped on at the moment of birth, in the way that newborn babies are tagged with name-bands.

Some of us are better parodists than others. Some, perhaps because of a neurological or biochemical deficiency, prove incapable of achieving the confident mimicry others acquire with relative ease. Yet even if you have managed to assume the superficial characteristics of an alien culture, the feat always retains some elements of parody. No matter how thoroughly you have been absorbed by your adopted society, and even if you have been accepted within its structures, as I have been, your otherness cannot be expunged. The last turn of the screw may well be that the more thoroughly assimilated you are and the more you come to think of yourself as an integral part of your adopted society, the more you are likely to be troubled by confusions of identity, by the anxiety of living in a vacancy between two worlds.

These paradoxes are frequently overlooked in the often simple-minded and pointless controversies about multiculturalism. One essential consideration tends almost always to be ignored. In the same way as it is impossible to become thoroughly assimilated, to wipe the slate clean at the moment of arrival in a new land, so it is futile to imagine that someone's heritage may remain entirely unaltered by a new environment. Preserving an 'ethnic' identity, in the manner implied by the propagandists of multiculturalism, may also be tantamount to cultural and social isolation. To encourage people to retain their native language is sensible for the simple reason that the more languages you know, the more open-minded, intellectually alert and perceptive you are likely to be. To put on your national costume and perform folk dances on the steps of the Opera House is, no doubt, great fun. The danger arises where such commendable and harmless activities are accompanied by attempts to lock people into ethnic enclaves or ghettoes, to seal them off from the society in which they must live, in the name of preserving an often dubious cultural heritage. I do not find it shocking that toddlers in the streets of Sydney should be heard babbling in outlandish regional dialects. But it is shocking that many of them, by the time they reach school, have acquired no more English than the phrases and slogans they have learnt from their daily bombardment by television.

It is not possible to achieve assimilation in the simple sense in which it was urged on us in those innocent days before politicians saw the prospect of enough votes to make them bother about us. Moreover, the impossibility of full assimilation has as much to do with the nature of Australian society—or indeed any society—as with the newcomers' predicament, their linguistic clumsiness, and their frequent prejudice against the people among whom they have chosen to live. I am not referring merely to the average Australian's unwillingness to accept anyone different, foreign and therefore deemed to be peculiar, though that was certainly a reality in the forties and early fifties, and is still to be encountered today. Rather, all migrants must face the insoluble problem of deciding which element of Australian society they should endeavour to join or adopt as a desired model.

A basic and fatally flawed assumption behind demands for assimilation is the fantasy that the society in which the newcomer has settled is uniform and homogeneous. Newcomers themselves willingly accept such myths because to them their bewildering new world inevitably seems harmonious, lacking in variety, tension or enmity. Recognising that the true state of affairs may be very different often takes considerable time. I cannot recall the exact point during the course of my education into Australian ways at which it became apparent that this world contained deep and unhealing scars. One incident nevertheless remains memorable because it revealed for me (and even more tellingly for my parents) that this seemingly uncomplicated and bland society was torn by passions of the sort that were only too familiar to people who had grown up in Eastern or Central Europe between the two wars. The shock of that recognition was sharper because it occurred not in one of those seething urban ant-hills of Europe, where political, religious and racial rivalries may so easily arise, but in a peaceful, sleepy and in many ways idyllic setting.

After several months of moving about in the inner suburbs of Sydney—a boarding house in Neutral Bay, two rooms with use of kitchen and bathroom in Hurlstone Park—my parents were lucky enough to find a self-contained flat in Epping, at that time more like a country town than a suburb of a large city. The flat itself was nothing much to speak of, no more than the perfunctorily converted servants' quarters of a handsome liver-brick bungalow, but in those days of acute housing shortages finding it represented a piece of extra-ordinary good fortune. One of its three rooms had no window but contained a large and entirely unusable fireplace. There was a kitchen and a lean-to, as well as a bathroom of sorts. The choko-covered dunny under a superb jacaranda proved a source of constant terror on account of its thriving colony of red-back spiders, which we were taught to disperse in the approved manner with a rolled-up newspaper. Nevertheless, securing that flat through the good offices of an acquaintance who had settled in Sydney some time before the war was the one bright spot in the otherwise bleak and depressing beginning of our life in the new land.

Nowadays Epping is a shrine to middle-class affluence. Its streets are paved and guttered; dunny-men no longer trot down its driveways with fragrant cans balanced delicately on their shoulders. Outside the primary school, where in the late forties one or two children still rode to school and tethered their horses to a hitching-post, a line of Volvos, Saabs and four-wheel drive monsters waits each afternoon for the class-rooms to disgorge their well-clad and properly shod young-sters. The shops nestled around the railway station display those heathenish goods—garlic-laden salami, capsicums, strange smelly cheeses—which, when I lived there, were almost entirely unknown: their gradual advance was greeted as the vanguard of the forces of darkness. Epping in the forties was, in other words, an example of an Australia which has disappeared entirely from Sydney, though I suspect that it survives in isolated pockets of Greater Melbourne.

To our European eyes it gave every indication of village life. In retrospect it is possible to be nostalgic about its sleepy charm, a quiet place where cows grazed in the paddocks behind several of the streets, a world where front doors were rarely locked, where you walked to school barefoot on hot bitumen, or in a sea of paspalum, wearing your threepenny imitation pith helmet. It was, nevertheless, a dreary place. Most of its handsome turn-of-the-century bungalows and two-storey houses were encrusted with fibro, corrugated-iron or timber excrescences: a verandah boarded up here, a lean-to added there. Elsewhere, weatherboard cottages leaned in various states of disrepair, victims of crumbling foundations, dry rot and termites. Only the gardens showed any signs of care and ownerly pride. And everywhere paspalum: the mile-long walk to the railway station (or at least as far as the few streets with properly made footpaths) had to be negotiated through acres of the weed which threatened to ruin your clothes with its burrs and oils, and harboured, besides, such dangerous nasties as ticks and snakes. The locals walked on the road; we had been too much regimented in our previous life to dare to do that.

Epping was at the time (and may well be still) the heartland of the nonconformist bible-belt. There was, it is true, a solidly constructed Church of England not far from the shopping centre, but the true spiritual aspirations of the place were represented by the Methodist, Baptist and Congregational establishments. One neighbouring family seemed to spend its entire Sunday walking back and forth between their place of worship and their house-cum-chicken-run at the bottom of a very deep battle-axe block. Sunday schools and youth fellowships flourished. The School of Arts in the shopping centre represented the secular arm of this firmly entrenched tradition: it provided a venue for various Lodges and Orders, into one of which I was briefly inducted as a teenage aspirant, in a ceremony that bore some resemblance to an amateur performance of *The Magic Flute*.

To us outsiders, all this appeared homogeneous and harmonious in its blandness. Here was a world of prejudices, perhaps, but one entirely lacking passion—or so it seemed. Its prejudice against us, who had strayed into this Arcadia from another planet, was essentially unmenacing. The crone who screeched obscenities at us over the picket fence of her tumbledown cottage was much too decrepit to offer any threat of violence and, besides, she had the reputation of being off her rocker—the children of the neighbourhood were convinced she was a witch. Passions, and indeed hatred, were reserved, as we came to learn, for others.

Our street was a broad roadway running for several miles bordered by the obligatory unmade verges and miniature fields of paspalum. It was, however, sealed as far as the point, a few houses beyond our place, where it took an abrupt ninety-degree turn. There the dirt road began. I do not know what bureaucratic decisions determined this highly symbolic frontier, but the distinction was very real. Beyond the curve, along the dirt, the houses were smaller, meaner and in even greater disrepair. The families living in them were larger, their front yards showed none of the care over clipped hedges and neatly swept driveways that distinguished the world of the bitumen.

We were too ignorant to read these signals. I made friends at school with two boys called Dunnicliffe, victims of scatological jests which, at first, I could not understand. They were the youngest in a large family that lived beyond the curve. I do not think we had much in common—how could we have had?—but no doubt we were drawn together because they too were shunned by the other children, just as I was after the initial impact of my arrival in 5B had worn off. This desultory friendship advanced a step or two when the Dunnicliffes arrived unannounced one Sunday afternoon. This was something quite beyond our experience. In my very early childhood when social life of a sort was still possible in a Hungary largely protected from the worst effects of war, social contact with other children was governed by a strict protocol of invitations and supervision. The Dunnicliffes said that they had come to play. We went into the paddock at the back, and played—as far as my still very limited command of English and of the mythology of Australian children's games permitted. They reappeared the following Sunday and then spasmodically throughout the summer holidays.

My friendship with these boys led to an incident which was our first significant insight into Australian society. Until then our relationships with our neighbours, with Australia as a whole, had been fleeting and sporadic—a halting conversation here, a hastily flung insult there. We had been living in a dream. People, places, events floated in and out of our experience without much impact. We observed the world of Epping from the outside, separated from it by an almost impenetrable screen. My father used later to say it was like watching a film you couldn't entirely follow. But the confrontation brought about by the Dunnicliffes' visits began to lead us inside a world from which we had been until then almost entirely isolated. There occurred, in short, some form of interaction between us and the people among whom we lived. Their world demanded a response from us, and consequently, for the first time, we found ourselves in a relationship with this society, and in a situation where, in theory at least, we were required to exercise some choice. Here was, in other words, our first real step towards assimilation, even towards becoming 'Australians'. But at the time the incident was merely an embarrassment, an awkward situation, and also an alarming recognition of the complexity of a world that had seemed until then quite simple and untroubled.

Our landlord was a mild-mannered man, a second-generation Australian of solid Lancashire stock, bearing a distinct resemblance to the King according to the women of his family. He spent most of the day pottering around in the backyard, tending his ducks and bantams. We did not know and never found out (such was our isolation in this world) whether he ever had an occupation. One of his three children, the eldest, lived at home (mostly in a chenille dressing-gown) because she suffered from 'nerves'—the consequence of an unfortunate marriage. They were an orderly family. Voices were never raised, speech never strayed beyond the laconic. Their days were largely governed by the wireless: *The Lawsons*, the news (for the war had established habits that proved hard to break), Mo and young Harry, and the Sunday night play.

One day our landlord knocked on the glazed door of the kitchen, the only entrance to the flat, having been no doubt egged on by his wife, a lady of much stronger personality, to remonstrate with my mother over the defilement of their Protestant paddock, if not home and hearth. For, of course, the Dunnicliffes were Catholics, as were most of the people who lived beyond the bitumen. My mother's surprise—once she understood what it was all about, after I had been fetched to do a spot of interpreting—was genuine, especially since for Hungarians (at least in our usage) the word 'Catholic' was barely if at all distinguished from 'Christian'. We knew that our landlord and his family were churchgoers, so what could all the fuss be about? At length my mother understood: being Catholic here was not all that different from being Jewish in Mitteleuropa. She accepted, it goes without saying, our landlord's ultimatum: either I was to tell the Dunnicliffes to stop coming around, or he would have to ask us to find somewhere else to live. As it turned out we did not have to do anything: the word must have travelled down the grapevine, for the Dunnicliffes never came again, and by the time we had gone back to school, they had found someone else to play with.

I have dragged this anecdote out of a confused array of memories not in order to draw analogies between Australian and European instances of intolerance and prejudice—for this minor comedy of bigotry pales into insignificance beside the brutality of the world we had left—but rather to illustrate how my first tentative and largely unconscious steps towards assimilation inevitably put me off-side with the dominant force in this little society. I had, entirely unwittingly, begun to align myself with people who were not acceptable to the tight proprieties of nonconformist Epping—families, like the Dunnicliffes, of Irish-Catholic ancestry, whose forebears had come to Australia as convicts, as seekers after gold, or else, like us, to escape a desperate and brutal world in search of security and immunity from persecution. The Protestant population of Epping, as of most parts of Australia, prided itself on descent from free settlers. Many years were to pass before it was chic to have convict blood running through your veins. In attempting to penetrate the social fabric of a world where my parents and I were considered outsiders, I had been attracted to a group within that community which was, for very different reasons, also excluded from full membership— they lived, after all, beyond the end of the bitumen.

In this way the doctrine of assimilation was given the lie (as retrospect clearly tells me) at a very early stage of my halting attempts to become a paid-up member of Australian society. People like us were urged on all sides to try to become good Australians. But one fundamental question was left unasked: what sort of Australians were we to become? What would being a New Australian (the cant phrase of the sixties) entail? Should you attempt to align yourself with Irish-Catholic Australia and its (to the newcomer) largely incomprehensible mythology of ancient wrongs? Or should you try to throw in your lot with what Manning Clark referred to as the Protestant Ascendancy? Should you become working-class or middle-class? The possibilities were and are numerous. The demand that newcomers must assimilate, promoted at the time when Australian society began to realise that it harboured considerable numbers of 'DPs', 'refs', 'balts', 'dagoes' and 'wogs', was entirely self-defeating.

Nobody seemed to realise at the time (or was prepared to admit in public) that assimilation could well become a two-way process. The emphasis was always on the newcomer's obligation to merge into Australian society, to adopt its ways, to learn the customs of the country, without in the least altering established patterns of behaviour, religious practice or communal ethics. The possibility that the migrant population might in some ways change the face of Australian society was generally feared. Programmes of assimilation were seen, consciously or otherwise, as insurance against such an eventuality. Nevertheless, the arrival of large numbers of migrants inevitably influenced the country's way of life. On the surface Australia seems to have eagerly embraced foreign habits and tastes. Yet underneath the old suspicions linger— even when they are expressed in terms of fashionable environmental and ecological concerns. Many people lament the passing of the old Australia. I know an elderly lady who is greatly distressed that you can't nowadays find a restaurant in Melbourne which serves what she calls decent Australian food.

The days of assimilation, at least as far as official policy is concerned, are long gone. Multiculturalism is the doctrine of the time. I find it curious and not a little amusing that, having been urged for many years to put aside my foreignness, I am now sometimes censured for having neglected my 'ethnicity'. But that, in turn, raises another issue. The doctrine of multiculturalism rests on the dogmatic basis that newcomers to this counry must not be forced, as they had been in the past, to discard their rich cultural heritage in favour of a possibly futile attempt to adjust their way of life. The dangers inherent in encouraging such a potential ghetto mentality are menacing and should not be left unquestioned. Moreover, advocates of multiculturalism have given birth to a highly misleading and inaccurate mythology concerning the aspirations of people who came to find a refuge, safety and a new home in this country; it involves the notion of coercion, symbolised by an image of hapless migrants, desperate to retain their characteristic ethnic headdress, cuisine, social rituals or whatever, being forced by the jackbooted agents of conformism into adopting Australian norms.

Since 1788 most people have come to this country under some form of compulsion—at first because they were convicts or were conscripted to become their gaolers, later to escape famine, hardship or persecution. In the worst days of the Cold War English families fled to Australia to escape the prospect of thermonuclear annihilation. But for many of them the compulsion was not sufficiently strong: after a couple of years they decided that the threat of extinction was preferable to their being denied what they saw as the civilised amenities of life—ranging from fish and chips wrapped in newspaper to the Royal Opera House, Covent Garden. Those migrants who stayed here, often because there was no possibility of return, and attempted to make a go of it, were usually impelled by nightmarish memories of the dreadful world they left behind. For my parents, initially at least, Australia was paradise. It may have been a curious and perplexing place, but it offered considerable safety and very little menace. If the worst that could happen to you was to have 'Go home, bloody ref!' shouted at you in the street, then the worst was good enough. The boring blandness of suburban Sydney was the guarantee they had been seeking. Surely, you could never have concentration camps in a place like this. Australia was a haven, a blessed land that seemed miraculously to have escaped the evils and the horrors of the old world.

For that reason, despite a sense of strangeness and perplexity, my parents were only too prepared to admire the world in which they had chosen to live; they were eager in their desire for acceptance. They knew in their heart of hearts that they would never become more than passably proficient in English. They also came to realise that they would always hanker after the world they had lost—a world which, they reminded themselves, had ceased to exist in 1939: a world, moreover, where they had witnessed brutality of a sort that could not possibly exist in these enlightened modern times, or so they had imagined. In their eyes, assimilation became not something imposed on them by a threatening and hostile society, but a desired goal, an aspiration which could never, alas, be fulfilled.

Along with that desire, bred out of gratitude and a sense of relief, went an unrecognised but, I think, deeply felt wish for something which was in essence nothing other than the desire for oblivion, the annihilation of the personality. This disturbing state of mind arose because they were only too conscious of what, in later years, was to become a recurring theme for discontent—the strangeness of Australia, an unfamiliar society which they came to regard as culturally impoverished. If only they could forget what they had lost. If only the past, the good together with the appalling, could be wiped out, then surely happiness and contentment would be theirs. They wanted to be remade, knowing all along what an impossible desire that was. They could not, of course, be refashioned. Freedom and security were theirs, and that was almost enough to compensate. Yet it was not quite enough. Though willing to become Australians—even if that were to prove impossible—those old habits, the familiar comforts of a very different world, could not ultimately be suppressed.

As time blunted their sense of relief and gratitude, and as the irritations of their life in Australia came more and more to grate on them, so dissatisfaction, frustration and nostalgia (which increasingly saw the past in a rosy glow) came to dominate their lives. They entered into a spiritual and social no-man's-land, citizens of no nation except by name and by the legal fiction of naturalisation—a predicament I have, to some extent, inherited from them. Long after their deaths, at a time when I have spent by far the greater part of my life as an Australian, I am still conscious of how fragile and provisional is the identity which I carry on my passport. Yet that other world, Europe—to which I am drawn by my instincts, my preferences, indeed by my inability, after so many years, to come to terms with Australian heat and humidity, for instance—seems to me as alien and as perplexing as were my first glimpses of Australia in the summer of 1947. That sense of dislocation colours these reminiscences in their attempt to lay troublesome ghosts, and to come to a better understanding of the world in which I have spent most of my life.

OVER
THE
RAINBOW

In 1946 my parents were preparing to emigrate to Australia. They spent long hours in queues waiting to be interviewed by stony-faced officials for exit permits and entry permits, for passport clearances and transit visas. One afternoon they took me to see *The Wizard of Oz*, a film which had been banned in Hungary (together with all American films) during the war years. There was no particular significance behind their choice; we often went to the cinema in that year. They merely wanted me to see a film they thought I would enjoy. Many years were to pass before that particular visit to the cinema would assume a retrospective irony. At the time Oz was nothing other than the place at the end of the yellow brick road. We were nevertheless soon to embark on a voyage that we thought might lead us somewhere just as remote and fabulous. My parents did not suspect that their journey could also end in a place as gimcrack as the mountebank's tent Dorothy discovers on the other side of the rainbow. Or if they did harbour fears and premonitions, they never spoke about them.

A great deal has been written about the migrant's experience of Australia, but relatively little attention has been paid to the aspirations and fantasies that prompted large numbers of people to undertake what was for them, quite literally, a voyage to the other side of the world. The migrant's predicament, which is that of the exile and the outcast, begins long before the moment of arrival in the new land. It is impossible to understand the anguish of alienation, perplexity and suffering—topics that have become parts of a minor mythology—without recognising those often contradictory forces that impelled people to take such large steps, to reach what was for many of them a frighteningly irrevocable decision. Each individual migrant's case is unique. Yet in the final count all these stories are the same story. Our experiences are typical, in broad pattern if not in fine detail, of the fortunes of those who went in search of the end of the rainbow to make a fresh start from the ruins of an older life.

What we found at the end of the rainbow was the most commonplace of images. Australia will always be represented for me by that first glimpse—a row of streetlights strung along a low hill, seen in the early dawn of a February morning. This image has haunted my imagination for almost half a century. It has become for me the essence of Australia, even though my rational self knows that such a very ordinary emblem cannot adequately reflect the varied and contradictory facts of a land or its inhabitants.

I saw those lights—the crest of Watsons Bay as I was to learn later—from the deck of the *Marine Phoenix*, a decrepit World War Two hospital ship, hastily refitted and reclassified as a 'Matson Liner', which plied between Sydney and San Francisco in the years immediately after the end of the war in the Pacific. It was the early morning of 21 February 1947, marking the end of our journey which had begun three months before in a freezing Budapest, a febrile, near-hysterical city trying to recover from the worst effects of air-raids, bombardment, occupation, disease and hunger. Here was the promised land, the gateway to the new life my parents had dreamt about through the darkest days of the war. After an extraordinary gamble (one shared by every migrant) and a long, difficult journey undertaken by people who had never travelled widely, the goal was this—a string of lights on a low hill.

Even if the Heavenly City had opened its gates to us as

the *Marine Phoenix* made its way up the Harbour, the disappointment would not have been any the less poignant. Journey's end is boredom, frustration and anxiety. The traveller whose jet sets down at Heathrow or Kennedy after a seemingly interminable flight knows that feeling of flatness. Was it worth all the bother just to come to this? We, too, asked ourselves that question on that morning, and on many subsequent mornings. Given the circumstances of our journey and the doubts and uncertainties surrounding my parents' decision to leave their familiar world—no matter how appalling it had become in the course of the previous decade— that numbing flatness, compounded of disappointment and fear, and exacerbated by the necessity to face the consequences of such an irrevocable decision, conferred on our arrival an exceptional and almost intolerable sense of weariness and despair.

An hour or so later we were lined up on the deck, our sleeves rolled back for the inspection of vaccination marks. Above us in the bright sunshine we caught sight of the arc of the Bridge, the one public image of Australia known to us, flanked by squat buildings with red roof-tiles. Scattered here and there were stands of scrawny trees that looked for all the world like overgrown broccoli. Another hour, and we had disembarked into a dreary, unimaginably hot shed, an ugly utilitarian edifice—one of the finger wharves at Woolloomooloo—amidst a throng of sweating, excited people. Tearful war-brides, bursting out of their smart New Look clothes, many of them carrying infants in those curious shoulder-slung canvas carriers which vanished mysteriously after the early fifties, were greeted by their bemused relatives—those who had said farewell to them, not many months earlier, when these young women set out (often on the same ship) to join their American 'husbands'. An important executive of Coca-Cola, whose family had occupied the only private cabin on board, while the rest of us were accommodated in dormitories of three-tier bunks, was surrounded by a gaggle of obsequious company officials. And scattered in this crowd, a handful of reffos,

19

wogs, balts, DPs like us, in our strange clothes, with our
equally curious gestures and demeanour, were being reunited
with our embarrassed, thoroughly 'Australian' relatives—who
were no doubt beginning to wonder whether it had been wise
to sponsor these odd remnants of a discarded way of life.

We had come to that finger wharf through a combination
of folly and courage, of hard-headed realism and romantic
self-indulgence. We followed the dictates of a seemingly
impeccable logic which was nevertheless based on absolutely
false assumptions. Family mythology always insisted that my
parents had intended to emigrate to Australia in 1937. They
saw what was coming. Their affluent and comfortable life—
all the more precious because they were the first among both
their families to enjoy such affluence and comfort—was
threatened on all sides. The atmosphere of Hungarian political
life was growing nastier each day. This was no place for a
family whose surnames told all: Riemer, Neubauer, Weiss,
Schillinger—not a decent Magyar name among them. In the
world outside, the ambitions of National Socialism were
apparent to all. But, the mythology continued, there was a
child to be considered; was it safe to underake a journey of
such hazards with an eighteen-month-old? An eminent paediatrician was consulted. His verdict was unambiguous:
travelling was out of the question, my parents must postpone
their plans for at least a year. By the following year the
unthinkable had occurred: Austria had been reunited with her
historic German heritage. To leave Hungary, that threatened,
landlocked little country which had always reacted nervously
to events in the world outside, became all but impossible. Or
so the myth insisted.

How much truth there was in all this I shall never know.
It would have taken prescience of an extraordinary sort to
foresee the state of affairs that was to exist by the spring of
1938. Yet many people had precisely such prescience. They
got out. We stayed. The next seven years proved to my parents
the extreme folly of their decision. They realised too, I think,
that the paediatrician's verdict may have been a convenient

lifeline; they had clutched at it eagerly because it gave official sanction to their inertia. They must not be judged too harshly. It takes greater courage than most comfortable middle-class people possess to cut all ties in the firm conviction that a stable and familiar world will soon vanish. At any event, my parents stayed. The consequences of their miscalculation ultimately proved to them the error of their judgment. And so, when they came to find themselves among the relatively few surviv-ors—everyone else in my father's family had perished—they attempted to make good that folly. We were among the first to leave Budapest.

Why did they choose Australia? There are three answers to that question, each of them highly significant in its individual way. The first was based on purely practical grounds. One of my father's cousins had lived in Sydney since the early thirties; before the war, he had written encouraging letters about the opportunities for migrants in Australia. The second reason was directly related to the first. My parents knew very little about Australia but they knew that the best wool in the world was grown there. That is where fantasy began to play an essential role. My father was a skilled textile designer. From the early thirties until the last phase of the war he had conducted his own business. He ran a small weaving mill which manufactured high-class men's suiting from the best worsted yarn in quantities sufficient to supply the fashionable bespoke tailors of Budapest and the larger provincial towns, with some exports to Vienna and Prague. Where else, then, to use his skill and knowledge to the best advantage but in the land where the wool he had worked with year after year was grown? What he did not know, but soon learnt to his cost, was that the comfortable world of bespoke tailors, unchanging designs of cloth—blue pinstripe, brown pinstripe, grey hopsack and the Austro-Hungarian version of tweed—supplied by small, specialised manufacturers was not a commodity much in demand in postwar Australia, if indeed it ever had been.

The last, largely unacknowledged, reason was, I think, the

most potent. It could not have been spoken about (at least until after the war) because it represented a fundamental desire or compulsion seemingly so irrational, so against the grain of good sense that one could not, in all conscience, talk or even think about it very much. It was simply this: to flee to a place as far away from Europe as possible, to find the antipodes in the full myth-laden sense of that word. My parents must have pored over maps often enough, they must have had the intuition that if they were to seek a world which would prove to be the converse of the horrors, injustices and brutalities of Europe, that unknown landmass at the southern and eastern extremity of the Eurocentric image of the world must answer their need. And in one sense they were absolutely right. To the ends of their lives, despite the disappointment, the frustration and the radical dislocation they had experienced, both of them retained considerable gratitude for the political freedom and security they had discovered in this curious land. Neither of them ignored—as I do not ignore—the fact that Australia was (and still is, though I sometimes wonder how long it will remain so) a liberal and generally tolerant society.

I do not wish to exaggerate or sentimentalise that sense of freedom and tolerance. People were often abominably rude, narrow and provincial, fearful and suspicious of our strange ways. Insults were hurled at us from the moment we set foot in Sydney. My first day at school is still painful to remember. These are instances of the crassness of Australian society which has become familiar from many migrants' reminiscences. It is entirely proper to register complaint, to point out that a society which prided itself on being almost exclusively Christian demonstrated precious little evidence of Christian charity. But the coin has another side. Though people were rude or insulting, they did not spit at you; they did not hurl bricks through your windows; you did not have to register your every movement with the police or the prefecture; no-one stopped you in the streets to demand your identity-papers; and certainly nobody battered on your front door with heavy fists in the dead of night. In comparison with much of the rest of the world, the essential health of Australian society in the years immediately after the war was remarkable. No amount of pettiness or small-minded meanness could tarnish it.

In the main, therefore, my parents acted wisely in seeking a new life in Australia. They found freedom and tolerance in this upside-down world where the outbursts of intolerance they encountered were often merely ceremonial. What they had not considered—or if they had, they dismissed the thought—was that they would find that there were certain aspects of this world to which they would never adjust. Australia, while offering us personal and political freedom, failed to fulfil a much deeper desire, a longing which gave birth to the fantasies we had fashioned out of a few scraps of knowledge and a great deal of wishful thinking.

We were woefully ignorant about conditions of life in a land that was not merely remote but had been isolated from Europe by the long years of the war and by primitive methods of communication. Most Europeans who made their way to Australia in the late forties were almost as ill-informed about the country where they intended to settle as were those who had embarked on such a journey in the nineteenth century. A few months before leaving Budapest we went to a cinema which, someone had told us, was showing a film about Australia. It turned out to be an item in an ancient newsreel. I cannot recall its subject matter. All I remember are three classical, clichéd images: a flock of sheep in a cloud of dust, a koala, and the Harbour Bridge. The koala was something new. With the addition of the kangaroo—and everyone knew about kangaroos—these images accounted for the sum of our knowledge of Australia. For the rest, we invented a paradise, a promised land, an El Dorado patched together from the dreams and fantasies of people living in a landlocked country of ice and snow.

My parents saw Australia as a balmy, tropical place beside an emerald-green sea. They imagined Sydney as a graceful Mediterranean pleasure-city (their model was no doubt picture-postcard views of Monte Carlo, Cannes or Nice) with palm-lined boulevards sweeping the curve of an ample bay. They saw white sand and, in the evenings, elegant, Latin-looking ladies and gentlemen sitting in the open-air cafés of these maritime boulevards. They saw sleek automobiles and many neon lights; they saw nightclubs with liveried doormen, and opulent restaurants. Somewhere, not far from this magical shoreline, they would find the opera house—for every large city had, it went without saying, its opera house. This would be, no doubt, like La Scala, the Met and the opera house in Budapest, but probably more splendid than any of those.

What does one wear to the opera in a tropical climate? they wondered—for air-conditioning had never entered into their scheme of things. Miraculously, my father still had some lightweight black material among his cache of prewar cloth, enough to make several dinner-jackets—he had wondered whether tails would have been more appropriate. My mother had a harder time: material for ladies' clothes was very difficult to come by. Fortunately someone knew someone else who had an American parachute for sale, and this provided enough silk, which could be dyed various colours, for three or four evening garments. My mother spent many hours with her dressmaker, a lady of alarming and probably phoney French accent, discussing what, precisely, should be made out of this marvellous cloth which had, so to speak, fallen out of the sky. Details of other clothes for Australia and for the last leg of our journey—first class from San Francisco on the Matson Line, we were assured—were worked out with equal care. Appropriate luggage had also to be ordered: light enough for the journey by air from Vienna to New York, but sturdy enough for use during the vacations we would no doubt be taking once we had established ourselves in Australia.

Then there was the matter of furniture. We assumed that we would be living in an apartment in a 'skyscraper': to an inhabitant of Budapest this meant a building of more than eight storeys. It would, of course, have a fine view of the bay, of the palm-fringed promenades with their cafés and elegant shops, and of the fashionably dressed ladies and gentlemen strolling beside the sea in the soft light of twilit evenings. How many rooms were there in a typical Sydney apartment? my parents wondered. Should they try to have some appropriately modern furniture made and have it shipped to Australia? Alas, neither suitable timber nor craftsmen reputable enough to be entrusted with the task could be found. They had to be content with my grandmother's family furniture, which, unlike their own, had survived the war—heavy Viennese pieces dating from the 1860s. Never mind, they thought, they could always get rid of the detestable stuff and buy something suitable when they knew what was needed—for there was never any doubt in their minds that they would achieve financial stability and success quite quickly, or that the money left over after the payment of fares and necessary bribes would multiply rapidly. As things turned out, that sum, about three thousand pounds, which would have been sufficient to buy a modest house in Sydney in 1947, thus removing an anxiety that tormented my parents for the next twenty years, disappeared within six months, my father having been expertly fleeced by several 'business associates' he had discovered among the newly-arrived migrants.

There was much speculation about the type of domestic help we would find. Did one have live-in servants or daily women? What colour were they? Were they usually negroes? I was reminded of that long-forgotten preoccupation many years later when visiting a lady my mother had known at school, who had been living in France since the early thirties. She told me how much she would love to visit us, to meet my mother again, but also to see those marvellous boats— what were they called? junks?—moored under the great bridge. There was a great bridge, wasn't there? It must be a wonderful place. Did we have very high fences to keep the kangaroos out? Did we have much trouble with our coloured servants? How many did we have? Were they honest, or did they steal food and clothing? Where did they sleep at night, in the house or in a compound?

It is easy to mock these fantasies—they were naive and self-

25

indulgent, and, worse still, they revealed the narrow insularity of Mitteleuropa's view of the world. People like my parents never looked beyond the confines of their restricted environment. They never entertained the possibility that elsewhere in the great wide world things might be ordained otherwise. They assumed that their priorities—based upon a bourgeois way of life in a society where labour was cheap and servants therefore plentiful—would hold good everywhere. They were, indeed, as ignorant about life in Australia as were most Australians about the nuances of European society. Yet these fantasies, the cloud-cuckoo-land they had invented, formed a crucially important element in the expectations they brought with them in their exile. They were to become the yardstick by which their experience of the new land was to be measured, even though it had been made to fit other standards. That is perhaps the most potent paradox in the migrant experience.

Elizabeth Jolley clearly understood that predicament in her story 'Paper Children', where an elderly Viennese lady travels to Australia to visit her daughter whom she has not seen since the child was smuggled out of a Europe about to burst into flames. When she arrives at her daughter's farm she finds an Arcadian idyll—or is it the most abject poverty? The daughter and her Australian husband seem to live in perfect amity; or is he brutal and heartless? Contradictory possibilities flicker over the surface of the story. Confused images of life in Australia clash and merge. But they are only fantasy-images fashioned in the last moments of the old lady's life: she had never set foot beyond her *gemütlich* Viennese world. Had she completed her journey, the reality she would have found would have been quite contrary to her fantasies, just as my parents and I found a world quite different from what we had expected when we disembarked from the *Marine Phoenix*.

Our fantasy-image of Sydney was quickly and irrevocably shattered once we emerged from the shed at Woolloomooloo into the dazzling sunshine. Yet such fantasies represent a fundamentally important facet of the newcomer's experience. They are an essential cause of a predicament all migrants must endure. My parents' childishly naive image of Australia was cobbled together from images culled from various films—usually with a Latin American setting—and from odd scraps of information picked up here and there. Their true source, however, was the fantasies entertained by people living in a landlocked country, who had never seen the open sea, who had encountered only stunted palm trees in a hothouse. Inevitably then, they imagined Australia, which they knew had a warm climate, as something of an amalgam of Carmen Miranda's Copacabana and Dorothy Lamour's Tahiti. Deep down, they were probably aware that the reality of Australia would turn out to be entirely unlike their dreams and aspirations. But they could not have imagined—even if they had been able to discard their Hollywood inspired vision of a South-Seas paradise—the extent to which their new home would contradict their cherished expectations. There remained, throughout their lives, something within their consciousness which whispered that it should have turned out otherwise, that, somehow or other, they had been misled and sorely cheated. This was not primarily a matter of external reality, of the stage-setting of their fantasies. It was, rather, a consequence of their inability to reconcile themselves to a world which ethically and socially, but also visually and architecturally, proved so alien and uncongenial to people who had never experienced the suburban sprawl of London, Manchester or Birmingham. They did not care for suburbia, and to the end of their days complained about its dullness, its lack of variety, its vistas of empty streets.

So powerfully ingrained within their consciousness was the image of European city-life that they conveniently forgot that they themselves had eagerly embraced a type of suburban existence in the first flush of their metropolitan affluence during the thirties. Some little time after I was born they gave up their fashionable rented apartment and bought a house—a 'villa' in the terminology of the time—in what they called a village and we would call a suburb, a short journey by electric train from Budapest. They thought that it was a very courageous and rather smart thing to do. No-one in the family had ever owned a villa, nor had an orchard of walnut, cherry, pear and apricot trees, as well as a small vegetable garden. While everybody had a maidservant, and some people could also afford to employ a cook, none of their acquaintances, confined to inner-city apartments, could boast a housekeeper (whose husband acted as part-time caretaker) living in a small self-contained flat in the basement.

It goes without saying that this village or suburb was a pleasant, leafy place, a Killara or a Kew, not at all like the ocean of red tiles you could see from the windows of our rented rooms in Hurlstone Park, or even the snake-ridden paddocks and paspalum-patches of Epping. Nevertheless, my parents' longing for the kind of urban life that Australia could not offer failed entirely to acknowledge that their happiest and proudest days were when they owned a villa out of town, when they could tell their friends that living there was not at all inconvenient—after all, the trains ran late into the night, you could easily get home after the theatre or the opera. Essential to their view of life was the irrepressible conviction that a city was only a city where people lived in apartment-blocks neatly joined one to the other, that a city which seemed to consist entirely of an expanse of sprawling villages had no right to call itself by that name. They longed for a world where you could go for a stroll in the evening to do a spot of window-shopping or meet your friends in a café, a way of life they had largely abandoned in order to immerse themselves in the joys of living in the 'country'.

Their disillusionment was in many ways inevitable, and it set in with remarkable rapidity. As the row of streetlights on the horizon drew closer, as the *Marine Phoenix* sailed past the headland, as the sun rose in a cloudless, pollution-free sky, and as we sweated our way through the interminable customs and immigration procedures, it was already establishing its grip on us. Once free of the wharf, we were bundled into our cousin's car, and made our way swiftly from Woolloomooloo to the Bridge through a Sydney ignorant of traffic-jams. What we saw was confusing and meaningless, lacking any context or point of reference, like a shadowy dream or a poorly edited film. Momentarily, a street which we came later to call Martin Place offered an urban vista we could understand; but then came the short stretch of George Street, its squat buildings with their menacingly disproportionate awnings, and very soon afterwards we were crossing the Bridge, travelling towards Cammeray and Northbridge.

'Is this a working-class district?' asked my mother, with the woeful lack of tact that was to prove in the years to come a frequent source of embarrassment, as we made our way up the hill towards the Suspension Bridge. The small brick or stucco houses, their fussy gardens, the general absence of street-life, the forlorn shopping-centres with their collapsing posts and awnings did not look like the kind of city my parents had expected. Where were the golden sands, the swaying palms, the elegant cars? Where was the promised land in which they would find not only political freedom, but that luxury and vitality which they had imagined from the grim perspective of a continent at war and a city under siege? Why wasn't this a happy and joyful land? In later years they were to ask the same questions in more complex ways. My parents grew, at length, to understand why Australians were not given to dancing in the streets, why their great ideal was to own a house with heavily curtained windows. Yet they never lost the feeling, which I have inherited from them, that this was a land of sleepwalkers.

I came to learn much later that such an attitude to life in Australia, no matter how hastily achieved, partial or unjust, is profoundly attractive to the displaced European sensibility. The image of a somnolent and anaesthetised land is powerful among European writers who have recorded their impressions of Australia. Lawrence's bleak vision in *Kangaroo* of a dreary Sydney, beyond which lay the threatening void of the bush,

Conrad's laconic comment in *Lord Jim* that this is *une triste ville*, or Anthony Burgess's remark that the sky above Sydney seems too innocent for crime or passion, represent Europeans' dismayed reaction to their first contact with the upside-down world. Australian writers are just as fond of using such images. Expatriates like Christina Stead or Shirley Hazzard, who look back from the perspective of the Northern Hemisphere on their early life in Sydney, and also those, like Patrick White, who made the difficult decision of returning to Australia, fill their books with those images of aridity, lack of passion and numbing propriety we fancied we saw in the Sydney of 1947.

As our cousin's car made its way through streets that, by European standards, were empty and drained of life, we began to wonder where the real city, the centre of its life, might be found. In *The Road from Coorain*, Jill Ker Conway writes eloquently about her first visit to Seville. She was amazed and enchanted to discover its great civic spaces—the cathedral, the plaza, the university—around which the life of the city turned. Here was something absolutely alien to her experience of city life—restricted as it had been to Sydney, Melbourne and Newcastle—an urbanity the like of which Australia could not provide. Though I could not have recognised it at the time, our first impression of Sydney was the direct opposite of the awakening that young Australian woman was to experience in Seville—we could find no physical, spiritual or social centre in a city which seemed to contradict all our notions of what urban life should be.

In later years, for people of my parents' generation, that image of deadness, of a world without a centre, came to be grafted on to another cliché about life in Australia which, curiously but significantly, also found expression in terms of space and of emptiness. The geographical void of a largely uninhabited continent—as seen from the perspective of the tight European world—the *horror vacui* Lawrence evokes memorably in *Kangaroo*, became transformed into the notion of a cultural desert. As the wave of Central European migration increased in the early years of the fifties, so that phrase and that concept were adopted and trotted out by people whose own cultural life had frequently not extended beyond the latest hit-play, movie or blockbuster novel. Yet, as espresso-bars began to sprout all over Sydney, so the lamentations about this horrible philistine place grew louder and louder. Where were the theatres? Ach, remember the opera (in Budapest, Vienna, Prague, Leipzig etc.). In the same way that many migrants automatically cranked themselves up several notches on the social scale, knowing that nobody could check on the extent of their confiscated estates that stretched, according to them, from horizon to horizon, so people began to lament the loss of those amenities which they had not much valued while they were available to them—the easily, at times glibly, invoked marvels of European high culture.

This attitude was often accompanied by a great arrogance—an arrogance that did much harm to emerging relationships between newcomers and Australian society. We were (I am speaking communally) only too ready to scoff and look down our noses on those poor antipodean provincials. That such attitudes arose out of fantasies and deeply mythic needs, rather than out of a just and balanced assessment of the nature of Australian society, was revealed to me with particular force in the London of the early sixties, when circumstances were forcing me to address myself to the difficult question of cultural identity.

Like so many young Australians—and by this stage I had come to think of myself as thoroughly Australian, until that illusion was totally shattered in the course of my first few days as a postgraduate student of English Literature—I was enchanted by the life London offered. You could hear great performers from the back row of the Festival Hall for five shillings; you could get a reasonable seat at Covent Garden for one pound. I lived near Selfridges, the department store, where the basement supermarket provided an ideal place to do the week's shopping on a Saturday morning. Around the corner, a little way up Baker Street, there used to be a curious establishment called the Balkan Grill. This was, despite its name, a typical Viennese Konditorei specialising in those oozingly baroque confections which are perhaps the old Habsburg Empire's most lasting contribution to world culture. After the exertions of shopping, I used to drop in at 'The Balkans', as it was known in the neighbourhood, for a cup of coffee. As I grew familiar with the place, drinking coffee became no more than an adjunct to the real purpose of the visit: to eavesdrop on the babel of Austro-Hungarian lamentations that filled the room. Ancient crones, their mouths grotesque scarlet gashes, sporting pearls and diamonds in almost obscene abundance, used to sit in their mink or Persian lamb coats drinking *Kaffee mit Schlag*, consuming lethal quantities of saturated fats, while they lamented the world they had lost, loud in their complaint that they were obliged to live in a cultural desert. Where was the music? Where was the art? Ach, where was the culture? And besides all this, why couldn't you find decent plumbing in this benighted city?

They were ridiculous and risible. London's cultural life was, at the time, probably the finest in Europe—more varied and of a higher standard than that of Vienna, Budapest, Prague or even Berlin before the war. But these sad and grotesque old ladies, reciting litanies which had probably lost all but their incantatory significance, were giving expression to their deep sense of loss. They were mourning a dead life. The 'cultural desert' of London was no more than a convenient counter to identify their sense of displacement, their longing for a past which could never be recovered. Seen from this perspective, London was as much a cultural desert as the most remote corner of Australia.

The tragedy of such lives is that an inevitable and natural nostalgia, an ever-present clog at the exile's heels, is invariably expressed in terms of comparisons and judgments which are made without much pertinence or justification. In a most important sense, such people have ceased to live; they are the living dead. What is different seems to them, naturally enough, inferior. A new environment, with its real or imagined disadvantages, is often blamed for the simple fact that people have been wrenched from the old. The agony of loss and longing casts a sentimental glow around what has been lost; it is always inclined to denigrate the new. We do not know how to recognise the benefits of a new world because the old has placed a template over our eyes—we perceive nothing except what those apertures allow us to see. Our lives are dissipated in longing and in the suffering of loss, even though what we have lost is only a country of the mind, a memory, or even a pure invention.

As we approached our cousin's house near a bushland reserve on Middle Harbour on that February day in 1947, the process I have been describing had already commenced. We were making comparisons between our old life and the new. And because we did not know how to make such comparisons, or on what to base our discriminations, we had begun in our arrogance and ignorance to judge harshly. To understand the source and the implications of those hastily achieved judgments—which I am still prone to make, long after I have come to realise that they are often partial and false—I must record what I can remember of our life before the moment of our arrival at the end of the rainbow, a moment which marked the cutting of our last ties with the past. Although my parents and I could have no way of knowing at the time, the instant we caught sight of those streetlights on a dark headland, our former life entered the realm of legend.

BEFORE
THE
FLOOD

Memory does not go back very far in a family like mine. Our story is a commonplace tale; it has been told many times. The broad chart of our particular fortunes nevertheless reveals something important about the perplexity of those people whose familiar existence was disrupted by the great upheavals of the middle of the twentieth century, who were obliged to remake their lives in circumstances that produced confusion, anguish and, for some, a debilitating sense of loss.

I know something about my grandparents, a little about my maternal great-grandparents, but beyond them there is nothing. Or rather, what came before must have been those inhabitants of the Austro-Hungarian world who were at one time Austrian, at another Hungarian, who may have lived in Bohemia, or in Moravia, or even outside the actual political confines of the Empire, perhaps in places like the Russian segments of Poland. In other words, though these people lived in and were no doubt citizens of the Dual Monarchy—the Imperial and Royal Austro-Hungarian Empire, to give it its most pompous title—they did not belong exclusively to any one of the various groups constituting that cumbersome, polyglot realm. They were neither Magyar nor Slav, neither Galician nor Ruthenian. If anything, they saw themselves as vaguely Austrian (even though in my father's family Hungarian was the first language), no doubt as a consequence of some sort of cultural osmosis of 'Austrianness' through the walls of one of the many ethnic, social or professional ghettoes which flourished in that complicated world. For all of them German was a *lingua franca*, establishing social, cultural and professional links, and providing for many of them the medium of their intellectual life. My father studied in Germany; my mother's family were primarily German-speaking—or, better to say, they spoke the outlandish dialect of a district known as Burgenland.

There had never been anyone famous in our family. On my father's side there was a half-hearted myth that we were somehow related to the Dr Riemer who was for a time secretary and factotum to the great Goethe—Thomas Mann depicts him as an unctuous, slimy pedant in *Lotte in Weimar*—but there is not, as far as I know, any shred of evidence to support this. Nevertheless, the fact that they entertained such a fantasy, even though in a half-serious, almost jesting fashion, reveals something important about their aspirations and their image of themselves. For such people, even a spurious connection with a 'famous' intellectual (in reality probably nothing other than an ill-paid and abused hack) provided quite a feather in the family's cap.

My father's people were thoroughly bourgeois, respecting rather than leading the life of the intellect. They had lived in Budapest for several generations. The men were usually engineers or held fairly important positions in various large companies. They made good marriages, often to quite wealthy women from a slightly higher stratum of society. My grandfather, for instance, was a sales executive for a firm of textile manufacturers. I do not think that he ever went from tailor to tailor hawking the company's goods, at least not by the time of his marriage, yet my grandmother always felt that she had married beneath her proper station.

I know next to nothing about her family except that her maiden name was Schillinger, and that she had a large number of sisters or female cousins who were either widowed or un-married, and spent most of their time gossiping or lamenting the cruelty of life. My grandmother was a great cemetery-goer. According to my father, she would never miss a funeral, even of someone only vaguely connected by ties of blood or acquaintance. The anniversaries of the deaths of the more important members of her family and circle were observed meticulously by ceremonial visits to various burial grounds. She gave birth to three children, a daughter and two sons, of whom my father was the youngest. Her life was not happy.

She was beyond any shadow of a doubt my favourite grandmother—largely because, unlike my maternal grandmother, she did not live with us. I remember her as a white-haired lady who always wore black dresses with white dots (except when in *grand deuil*) and lace-up boots. She had a wonderful china-cabinet filled with Dresden figurines, which I was never allowed to touch, and a collection of small silver objects—windmills, boats, cottages—with which I was allowed to play whenever we visited her. My mother used to say that her mother-in-law and my father's sister had initially resented her, the provincial upstart, but by the time of my earliest memories these resentments seemed largely to have vanished.

My grandfather died just before my parents' wedding. He had been separated from my grandmother for many years, living with 'a woman in Prague' (the phrase assumed mythic proportions in the family) whom he left once a year in order to accompany his wife and children on their annual holiday at a lakeside resort. These apparently were the conditions set by my grandmother before she agreed to a separation. Keeping up appearances was a quality about which my father cared little, but my mother instinctively understood its importance. For that reason perhaps, my grandmother and to a lesser extent my aunt came eventually to drop their early hostility towards her. Just before my parents were married, my grandfather returned to the bosom of his family to die.

My father had not made a 'good' marriage. Not that his family had any moral misgivings about my mother (at least as far as I know) but she suffered from serious disadvantages:

she came from outside their circle, and she was practically a pauper. This sounds a harsh and calculating attitude, and no doubt it was so to some extent. But behind its precepts lay decades of bourgeois prudence: keep within the known and trusted circle, do not neglect the necessities of life—if the man is capable of earning good money, his wife must bring some property to the marriage in order, as it were, to balance the books. Since the women in these families were relieved almost entirely of all responsibilities other than the supervision of housework, the concept of unpaid work as a contribution to a marriage, so often invoked by modern feminist theory, had little relevance for them. Such prudence is probably to be encountered in any propertied society, but in prewar Europe its practice had been refined into an art-form of elaborate conventions and rules of decorum. The first volume of Proust contains an account—at a much higher social and cultural level than my parents' world—of this ritual, which was conducted from one end of Europe to the other, and had spread throughout the spectrum of castes that constituted the bourgeoisie.

From the perspective of her in-laws, my mother was deficient in at least three important respects: she was provincial, she was an orphan (her father had died when she was very young) and she was very poor. Whereas my father's family had been city people for several generations, my mother was born in a village on the shores of a large, shallow lake that now forms part of the border between Austria and Hungary. The nearby town, where my mother grew up, was generally known as Oedenburg until 1921. After the Treaty of Versailles, a rather suspect plebiscite (in which the dead were said to have voted enthusiastically) decided that the town should be absorbed into the newly independent state of Hungary, and that it should be known exclusively by its Hungarian name, Sopron. As a means of rewarding the gallant (and largely German-speaking) citizens of Sopron for their courageously patriotic act, the Hungarian government decided to endow it with the title *Urbs Fidelissima*.

My mother was the daughter of a village schoolmaster who
died from meningitis when she was a toddler. My grandmother—a widow of twenty-two—left the schoolhouse and
went back to live with her parents. My great-grandfather,
whom I remember distinctly, was a little, compactly-built
man with pronounced Slavic cheekbones, despite the fact that
his name was David Weiss. He was something of a grandee
in the village. The caste-obsessed Habsburg world extended
its influence to the most obscure recesses of its domains. He
was involved in the dispatch by train of milk from the estates
of the great Eszterházy family to the two capital cities—
Vienna and Budapest. I do not know what my great-grandfather's function was—I think it may have been entrepre-
neurial. I do not think he was an employee of the railways.
I say this because this side of my family, though conscious
of its humble origins, habitually thought of itself as a cut
above the local peasantry and rural *canaille*. In earlier times
they may well have been servants of the Eszterházys or of
their retainers, for the one shred of mythology in that part
of the family concerned my great-grandfather's grandfather,
who was supposed to have 'known' Haydn during his years
as Kapellmeister at Eszterháza.

My great-grandfather saw himself as a person of some
importance; he took pride in the orderly flow of milk to the
great capitals. He considered himself, albeit in a small way,
an important part of the machinery that ensured the smooth
operation of that vast, benevolent Empire which was joined
by an unbroken chain extending all the way from the Kaiser
und König in Vienna to the humblest peasant on its eastern
extremity. He had a uniform and a braided cap to denote
his station along that chain. He has been given an immortality
he hardly warranted in an anecdote in David Malouf's
Harland's Half Acre. How mistaken he was in his faith in
the stability of the Habsburg world was proved to him a
few years after the birth of his first grandchild, my mother,
who was born in 1912.

Around the time of my mother's birth, when her mother,

the widow Neubauer, moved back to her parents' house after her pitifully short marriage to the village schoolmaster, this world seemed stable, comforting, eternal. Franz-Josef, the benevolent, avuncular monarch, still mourning (according to popular mythology) his assassinated Empress (even though they had, in fact, loathed each other), ruled over his people from the big city, Vienna, seventy or so kilometres to the west. For my mother's family Vienna was 'their' city. What you could not get done in nearby Oedenburg you could accomplish in Vienna, a short train journey away. When my grandfather began developing the symptoms of the meningitis which was to take his life, the doctors of Oedenburg decided that he must be taken to Vienna, where he died. My grandmother often spoke about his funeral in a cemetery on the outskirts of the city. She remembered her father in his splendid uniform and black armband, and how my great-grandmother had discarded for the occasion the black kerchief she wore every day of her life, replacing it with an ancient, heavily-veiled black hat. But this orderly life, with its dependence on the kindly monarch and the great city, commemorated in Robert Musil's wry masterpiece *The Man Without Qualities*, was not to last. It was shattered not so much by the Great War as by its aftermath.

After the disintegration of the Habsburg Empire, various provinces in Austria and Hungary were shaken by socialist, anarchist or bolshevist uprisings (the epithet varied from place to place). One of these forced my great-grandfather and his family (every one of them exploiters and toadies, of course) to take refuge in their cellar. My mother, who must have been six or seven at the time, recalled those days of terror more vividly and referred to them more frequently during her years in Australia than she was to speak about those later times, in the forties, when she was forced once again to seek shelter underground. They lost everything. According to my mother and grandmother, who saw all their woes as stemming from that time, the revolutionaries made off with considerable wealth: all their worldly possessions, furniture, clothes, sacks of produce, and most damagingly several bags of gold coins which had been carefully hidden in cunning places all around the house. Only one small satchel survived the attention of the raiders. A hitherto prosperous family was ruined. They were taken in by my grandmother's cousins who lived in Oedenburg (soon to become Hungarian and Sopron). Throughout my mother's childhood and adolescence these cousins took exquisite delight in reminding their impoverished relatives of their extraordinary kindness.

I remember some of these cousins, their children and their grandchildren, who were my contemporaries. These are among my earliest memories, and I believe that they have stayed with me all this time—when so much else has vanished—because it was my first experience of the subtle patterns of beastliness that govern family relationships. Each year until 1943, when Hungary became involved in the war in an immediate and disastrous way, we would visit our Sopron relatives at Easter-time. By this stage my mother had become the metropolitan grande dame, wife of the successful manufacturer (whom these people had remembered as the young manager of the local weaving-mill). We would descend in our smart city clothes, my mother swathed in furs, exuding cosmopolitan sophis-tication. The cousins were dowdy and provincial, and were made to feel so by my mother's account of life in the city—the theatres, the restaurants, her dressmaker, milliner, hair-dresser, our neighbours who drove a large black convertible (it was rare in those days for people to own motor-cars), and above all how one night the Prince and Mrs Simpson had sat at the table next to theirs in a fashionable Budapest nightclub (even though by the forties this anecdote had become rather stale).

A precise memory concerns a young cousin—I have long forgotten her name. She was sitting on one of those revolving piano-stools which was, that week, the envy of my life. Round and round she went, the gold ringlets of her hair flying past at ever greater speed. I felt anguish and despair—we did not have a piano, let alone a piano-stool. My spinning cousin was conscious of her power; waves of contempt flowed out of her twirling body. I could bear it no longer: I grabbed hold of one of the flying ringlets, and off she came, tumbling onto the Persian rug, howling in delight because she knew she had scored a considerable advantage over me. At that moment the polite beastliness conducted by the grown-ups over afternoon tea (a meal which always included all sorts of food and beverages except tea) erupted into open warfare. The cousins turned on my mother, accusing her of ingratitude, calling her an upstart, prophesying a horrible criminal future for me. Had not, after all, my mother as a girl scandalised everyone when she was seen by the whole town riding pillion on my father's motorbike? They had said it at the time, and they would say it again: she was shameless, and shameless people have shameless children. I have no recollection of what happened after that. Did the storm pass? I do not know and it does not matter very much, for all these people are dead and, if the dead live on, I hope against hope that they are not spending eternity reliving old squabbles and rivalries.

Oedenburg, Sopron, called Scarbantia by the Romans, represented one of the principal vantage points from which my mother judged the sprawling suburbs of Sydney. It was— I write in the past tense for I have not seen it for half a century, even though I tried in vain to find a night's accommodation there during the hectic Christmas season of 1990, when every expatriate seemed to be looking for hotel rooms all over Hungary—a town of about fifty thousand inhabitants nestled below some pleasant hills that briefly break the monotony of the great plain that begins to the east of Vienna.

As you leave Vienna, passing cemeteries, and a huge petro-chemical plant, the Austria of popular imagination, that is the Austria of *The White Horse Inn* and of *The Sound of Music*, is swiftly left behind. 'Asia begins at the back door of my palace in Vienna,' Prince Metternich is supposed to have said, and it is immediately obvious what he meant. For very soon signs of the Turkish invasion and occupation begin to appear. The farther you travel, especially after you cross that curious little puddle of a river called the Leitha, which served, incredibly, as the border of the Holy Roman Empire, you notice more and more remnants of Islam: bathhouses and the suspicion that some churches have done service as mosques. There are other signs of the past as well: Caruntum, a great Roman outpost, built, with the obsessive practicality of the Romans, in the middle of nowhere just because two great highways crossed at that point. There is also increasing evidence of that most Hungarian of emblems: tall farmhouse chimneys, each with its obligatory stork's nest.

Until very recently, as you continued along this highway, you came upon a wire fence, a watchtower, and an old woman scratching away at a cabbage patch. Not far from that fence, otherwise known as the Iron Curtain, you would soon come upon Sopron, itself an amalgam of Austrian, Turkish, Roman and Hungarian influences. Now the fence is gone. Sopron may, in years to come, begin to find again something of its identity as Oedenburg, a town sharing as much with Austria as with Hungary, a town that always looked towards Vienna, rather than in the direction of a distant and somewhat provincial Budapest. The mood in contemporary Hungary looks back with some nostalgia on its Habsburg past. But the people of Sopron are unlikely in the near future to run up to Vienna to do this or that, as my mother's family used to do—the problems of a soft-currency economy will prevent that.

My memories of Sopron are vague and discontinuous. Most vividly remembered is a curious, rough-hewn stone tower, built, I was told, on a Roman base, which had formerly served as a lookout to warn of the coming of fire or of invading hordes. This was, I think, the oldest part of the town, where there were other Roman remains, as well as bits and pieces revealing the influence of the Turkish domination of that part of the world, and beautiful timbered houses, modest on the street-side but displaying, through their arched gateways, glimpses of spacious courtyards surrounded by overhanging balconies with intricately carved decorations. Elsewhere, one could see that Vienna was not far away. I recall a large square with the municipal theatre at one end (where I was taken to see *The Gypsy Baron* on one of our visits) and nearby the vast Ursuline convent where my mother was educated. I have no recollection of any sort of cathedral, church, or synagogue though there must have been such establishments somewhere. But I do remember with some clarity the hotel where we used to stay, also situated on this square, which (memory tells me) was constructed according to the provincial's understanding of Viennese *luxe*, with elaborately moulded ceilings and crystal chandeliers.

The compact design of this little town suggested solidity and reliability. You knew where you were. Each part had a function, or at least a significance. Whether you regarded the square or the watchtower as your focus, the town made sense. Its variety testified to continuity—outliving the Romans, the Turks and, at least for Hungarian patriots, the wretched Austrians; its compactness spoke of a sense of community. I suspect that life in Sopron must have been deadly dull; but for my mother even that dullness came to seem rich and comforting when compared with the very different dullness of Sydney in the fifties.

Where Sydney differed so much was in its monotony. No Roman ruins, no Turkish remnants, no reminders of a Habsburg past, though one or two of the buildings in Macquarie Street were strangely reminiscent, in size and relative crudeness, of Sopron's attempts at Viennese grandeur. There was the unsettling sense that in Sydney people lived not in but around the 'city', which, we came to realise in the weeks after our arrival, was almost exclusively dedicated to the demands of commerce. We knew nothing about the social topography of Sydney suburbia; nor did we appreciate, as I do now, that those relatively few Sydneysiders who live around the shores of the Harbour lead a life no less attractively urban than the smart apartment-dwellers of European capital cities. What we were conscious of were the miles and miles of undifferentiated suburbs, rows upon rows of mean bungalows, stretching to the end of the world—or at least to the foot of the mountains—a depressing world of dormitories, where there was no reason to walk along the street unless you had to go 'out' to get something done. I do not think that this sentiment was misplaced: compared to the awfulness of Epping—especially when tinged by nostalgia for the irrecoverable—even the provincial boredom of Sopron was vastly preferable.

The Ursuline convent furnished my mother with another myth-world which was to colour many of her attitudes later in life, whether as the grande dame of Budapest or as the seamstress of Epping that she became for several years. Because of some obscure dispute with an Archbishop or even perhaps with the Holy See (my mother was always vague about the precise circumstances) the Ursulines of Sopron became a closed order. They retreated behind the walls of their handsome convent and continued the task of educating the young ladies of the district from a position of apparently total isolation. Though they were a Catholic order, they seemed remarkably generous in their acceptance of pupils of various faiths— Protestants as well as Jews—reflecting in many ways the attempts of the old monarchy to bring harmony to the many creeds amongst its subjects, even in the face of the antisemitism and other forms of bigotry that had always marred Austro-Hungarian social and political life.

They may have been a closed order, but they were by no means denied the amenities of life. I do not know how accurate my mother's accounts of the splendours of convent life were— quite possibly they were tinged with a certain romantic aura— but clearly the Ursuline ladies did everything to overcome the disadvantages of isolation. They were anything but self-lacerating anchorites. Indeed, the word 'ladies' was crucially important. They were ladies, many of them titled (though that did not signify much in a world which was very liberal with dispensing honours), who were required to bring a handsome dowry to the order. It was generally expected that they would also bring the benefits of a good education. Several were university graduates. They seemed to have retained considerable contact with the outside world. Visitors were received in what my mother described as an elegant salon. Parcels of the latest books from Vienna were constantly delivered to their front door. And they had one of the first wireless receivers in the town.

I do not know what passions and anguish marked the lives of these women, how many had immured themselves because of some grave disappointment in life, or if any had been incarcerated by their families for some terrible indiscretion. My mother never spoke of such things. But she did recall with great pleasure the few glimpses she was vouchsafed of their calm, orderly, and civilised way of life. No doubt that life seemed particularly glamorous to the impoverished orphan living in a poky flat, sustained by the charity of contemptuous relatives. She remembered the handsome, beautifully fur-nished apartments each of these ladies occupied, having brought with them not merely exquisite pieces of furniture, heirlooms of great value, but personal servants who became members of a lower—in truth menial—branch of the order. The emphasis was always on ease, on luxury, on elegance and even on sophistication, especially that typically European sophistication which sees the consumption of high culture (in carefully measured doses) as a necessary adjunct of the chic. Of their spirituality or devotion there never seems to have been a word. Their allure was purely secular and material.

Several years of exposure to this way of life probably implanted in my mother the desire to rise on the social scale. Her rapid transition from a relatively naive provincial to a metropolian sophisticate was prompted, I think, by what she saw—or fancied that she saw—while under the care of the Ursulines with their elegant quarters, their wireless sets, their important visitors, and their tennis courts which were made to freeze over each winter so that the nuns might go skating in their billowing black habits. They set my mother, wittingly or not, on an upward trajectory which was to crash painfully to earth in Epping in the forties, when she was obliged to learn to use an industrial sewing machine and seek employment at the tyrannical Miss Melville's clothing factory for a wage of seventeen shillings and sixpence per week.

Miss Melville's sweatshop lay, however, in an unimaginable future. My mother's road to social and economic advancement took another step when, while still at school, she met my father, at that time the manager of a textile-mill in Sopron. After a long engagement, bitterly opposed by their families (he was eight years older; she was considered a pauper), they were married in 1935 and established themselves in a modern apartment block in a fashionable quarter of Budapest. They were to have seven or eight golden years. My father's business prospered. In 1937, instead of emigrating to Australia, they purchased the villa in which they gave large parties that always came to an end with animated games of poker lasting until the first light of morning. They acquired at this time the most sophisticated of novelties, an electric record-player that plugged into a menacing radio-set with a complicated dial and a sinister green eye. A small espresso machine—another treasured possession—exploded at one of these parties, almost blinding my mother, and leaving an indelible brown stain on the ceiling. On New Year's Eve they used to melt the lead seals of champagne bottles and drop the molten metal into a vat of icy water in order to discover, from the complicated shapes that formed in those vats, what the coming year would bring. Around this time my mother went through a Spiritualist phase. She organised séances at which various notabilities, especially Marie Antoinette, caused the legs of a spindly table to tap. That obsession returned in a much grimmer form in the last months of the war when these shades were summoned to answer despairing questions—'Will we survive? When will it end?'—to which they always gave riddling answers.

It was a charmed life, perhaps a silly and self-indulgent life, but it was also pathetic in its brevity. It may have lasted a little longer than the good life enjoyed by people like them in other parts of Europe; Hungary remained relatively untouched by the war until 1942. Yet even after the bombing began, even after rumours were heard about people being rounded up in odd pockets of the country, my parents' nightclubbing and theatre-going continued, interrupted from time to time by my father's being called up, at first for military service, later on to join gangs of road-builders and ditch-diggers. Each time he came home—on one occasion as the batman of a monocled 'Excellency' who carried my father's kitbag to the front door of the villa, clicked his heels and kissed my mother's fastidiously manicured hand—the parties, the high time, began once more. Even so, their golden time was very short—by 1944 it had all vanished.

Yet these few years, with their echoes of the real or imagined splendour of the Ursuline way of life transferred to a brittle metropolitan setting, set the benchmark, the standards whereby my mother measured the rest of her life. In retrospect it seems a venal and shallow outlook. She possessed few intellectual capacities or ambitions. The apparently aimless life that took her from dressmaker to milliner, from morning coffee to lunch, from an afternoon at the cinema (or rather at one of the cinemas where it was fashionable to be seen) to meeting my father and several other couples for dinner was sufficient to satisfy her needs. Though my parents went regularly to the opera I do not think that she had ever attended a concert or a recital. Even the opera bored her, unless it was *Carmen*, *La Bohème* or at a pinch *La Traviata*. But she enjoyed sitting in the box every Wednesday night during the season, casting a critical eye over what the other ladies were wearing, just as she always attended performances of long-running plays whenever notices appeared in the papers announcing that the leading lady had been fitted out with an entirely new wardrobe of costumes.

She may have been a less than ideal mother. I was left largely in the care of a succession of German nannies (all of them answering to the no doubt generic name of Tante

Anna) with my maternal grandmother, a rather sour soul, acting in a supervisory capacity. I would see my mother briefly in the morning before she went into town, and in the afternoon as she was about to change for dinner. Yet my parents were neither uncaring nor basically irresponsible, and certainly not vulgar—although it may be that I am too partial to be reliable on that last point. They had a measure of style and elegance— even though it was newly acquired and thinly applied. Again, I must be scrupulous in declaring possible partiality, but my mother seems to me to have avoided, then and later on, the crass vulgarity of those Hungarian ladies of Double Bay, with knuckleduster diamond rings and bracelets like the wristbands of a heavyweight wrestler, who talked at the tops of their voices in a barbaric tongue, or else slaughtered Australian-English in a way which was easy to parody. My parents were no doubt *nouveaux riches*, but they carried their new-found (and sadly temporary) wealth with some taste and discrimination.

I know much less about my father's family. This is so partly because he was naturally reticent, not a born myth-maker like my mother. It may have had something to do with a reluctance to speak about my grandfather's defection, though in his last years my father mentioned it quite frequently. He seemed to bear his father no grudge, only a regret, perhaps, for my grandmother's distress. The fundamental reason, though, why a mythology had not been elaborated in that family—apart from the half-jesting tale of Goethe's friend and factotum—was their ordinariness. They were absolutely typical of a very large element in that Central European bourgeoisie which was already beginning to disappear by the time the war saw to their extinction. Apart from my grandfather's peccadilloes, nothing remarkable seemed to have happened to them for generations. Nothing had disturbed the pattern of their commonplace and predictable lives, in sharp contrast to the fortunes of my mother's family, who had suffered grievously during the disintegration of the Habsburg world.

I did not know my paternal grandfather. After his death a few months before my parents' wedding, his widow remained in the family flat in an unfashionable part of Budapest where she had always lived as an abandoned wife, consoled by my uncle, her unmarried son, and my aunt, who was married to a wholesale dealer in horseflesh. Though I have no clear memories of my uncle or of my aunt, I remember vividly the dealer in horseflesh. He was very tall and fat, with a shaved head. He terrified me—entirely without cause—and consequently the anticipation of pleasure every time we set out to visit my grandmother was tarnished by childishly irrational fears. Of my grandmother's flat I recall no more than her china cabinet and collection of silver bibelots, and that the polished floors were covered with rugs. I still have some of her rugs, and much of her furniture—but not the fabled china cabinet—though I have no recollection whatever of these pieces in their original setting, where I must have seen them every time I was taken to visit her. One tiny scrap of memory fits somewhere into this sparse picture. There was a coin-telephone in the flat. You had to insert a coin and push a button before the telephone could be used. My father used to say that it entirely failed as an economy measure because each time members of the family wanted to make a call, they opened the container, extracted the single coin it invariably harboured, and fed it again to the hungry machine.

My grandmother owned or at least had a major interest in the small block of flats where she lived. This was the source of her income and also the centre of her social life. Most, perhaps all, of the other apartments were occupied by members of her extensive network of family and close friends. Her own apartment was the venue for gatherings of elderly ladies—sisters, cousins, widows of cousins, cousins of the widows of cousins and so on. Her flat was also the location for less frequent but larger gatherings of what must, I suppose, be called the clan. Once more, my memories of these celebrations are indistinct, except that I still bear the stigma of one of those occasions, when I crashed head-first into the china cabinet and had to be rushed to hospital for stitches. The accident seemed to have left me unscarred, until in middle-age a vertical furrow suddenly appeared above my right eye, a revenant from a dead world, a living *memento mori*.

One of the established members of this clan, that spread beyond immediate family ties to encompass intimates and associates linked by friendship or marriage, was an elderly bachelor, a meticulously dandified gentleman who always wore spats. He was a retired town clerk, and had been, on his retirement, granted some honour appropriate to civic functionaries. He insisted on being addressed, even by people like my parents and grandmother, with the full honorific, and would fly into furious rages if anyone dared to omit the 'Excellency' to which he was entitled. He also had very pronounced views concerning propriety. I recall one terrible scene during one of his visits to our villa in which he berated my mother because she painted her nails. I could not understand at the time why my parents were so upset by this incident, why they severed relations with this gentleman for many months until he offered a grudging apology, for in that world people constantly criticised each other openly and with considerable verbal violence. His behaviour seemed to me no different from everyone else's. Much later, I learnt that his offence was to stray beyond the strict boundaries that this society had imposed on such acts of reprobation: he had said that my mother looked like a whore. That was beyond the pale. Had he not said that, he would have been permitted to continue with his reproaches, growing increasingly more strident and even insulting, without anyone's turning a hair.

Such were the anomalies of that world—on the one hand rigid probity, on the other licence for considerable vehemence and even for a degree of coarseness which would not at that time have been tolerated in Australian society. The small gatherings and the larger celebrations in my grandmother's flat would display the two contradictory poles of this social phenomenon: ceremonial and at times openly hypocritical *politesse* and violent, often quite coarse, invective. His bespatted Excellency, the retired town clerk, would gallantly kiss the hand of each dumpy crone, complimenting her on her beauty and youth. The company would then proceed to indulge in delicious gossip, slander and innuendo, with liberal use of the scatological richness of the Hungarian language, tolerating considerable vulgarity of expression in what was regarded as polite society. The only instance of such a mixture of urbanity and indecency I have encountered in English culture is in the patrician world depicted in the comedies of Congreve and his contemporaries. This social mode, which flourished among the bourgeoisie of Hungary, and may still be heard in public places like the foyer of the Sydney Opera House, though it is notably absent in the Budapest of the 1990s, was probably the remnant of a former way of life where the rural gentry lived in close contact with the peasantry. But that is sheer conjecture on my part.

My grandmother's flat formed the centre of her life—at least in the years that I knew her—in a way completely opposite to my parents' gadding about from restaurants to nightclubs during their golden years. She rarely went farther than visiting friends and relatives who lived in the same building or in nearby streets, except for those frequent and highly ritualised trips to the cemetery that played an essential role in her life. Domestic duties occupied a great deal of her attention—she had after all three adults living with her—but these were of an exclusively supervisory nature. There was a live-in servant who, in the manner of these bourgeois households, was combined cook and chambermaid. The laundress came each Monday. A dressmaker would call from time to time and sew on my grandmother's treadle machine (which she herself never used) that succession of black dresses with white spots, in cotton, silk and wool, which my grandmother wore each day. A lesser creature would attend to such mending as was not trusted to the maidservant. The corn-cutter (no fancy terms like chiropodist or podiatrist were then known) would come whenever necessary, as would someone with leeches or cups for those minor medical matters that did not require the services of a doctor. If a doctor were needed he (for no woman doctor could be trusted) would also call—a visit to the consulting-rooms was reserved for the gravest of maladies, when the opinion of a specialist, inevitably a Professor, was called for. My father used to say that when he was a child, a person (some sort of minor, possibly untrained dentist) would be summoned if a tooth needed extracting.

I do not remember a piano or a radio or a gramophone or any books at all. Yet my father was relatively well read, and he was very musical indeed, though entirely as a listener, despite several agonising childhood years at the violin. I suspect that he acquired these tastes when he left home after finishing his schooling. He spent some years studying to become a textile engineer, first in the Czech city of Brno, later in Aachen in Germany. It was during his years in Aachen that he used to travel all night in a third-class compartment to cities like Dresden and Leipzig to queue for most of the day for an opera ticket, only to return to Aachen by the late train, sleepless and exhausted. His musical interests were restricted to opera; he spoke of some legendary singers he had heard. He would occasionally mention the odd conductor, principally Strauss, whom he had heard conducting a performance of *Der Rosenkavalier* in Dresden or Leipzig. He never spoke about orchestral concerts or chamber music recitals. Nevertheless, his cultural horizons were wider than my mother's. He had seen something of Europe. After he had finished school his mother stood him a trip to Venice, where he stayed with a reliable and respectable Hungarian family who fed him proper and decent food. A few months later, before beginning his studies, he used his meagre savings for a visit to Paris—a three-night journey in third class—where unfortunately a reliable Hungarian family could not be found. To my grandmother's dismay he slept in an hotel and ate goodness knows what muck in cafés and restaurants.

In this account of the two sides of my family I may have stressed the differences in the way each looked at the world. But such differences are probably more striking in retrospect than they were in fact. They each remained fixed within fairly clearly defined boundaries, the boundaries of a bourgeois world where certain proprieties were carefully observed, even though people of my parents' generation often exercised greater licence than their elders thought proper. Though my parents enjoyed in their few years of relative peace and prosperity the amenities of a 'fast' way of life, there was little if any sexual indiscretion among their friends. Indeed, men of my grandfather's generation were much more likely to succumb to a 'woman in Prague' than those of my parents' nightclub-going, relatively hard-drinking circle. Divorce was almost unheard of. Children were generally cherished. Their welfare was a constant preoccupation, so much so that many were smothered by a possessive and over-protective love.

My mother's leaving me largely to the mercies of nannies and governesses was quite normal according to the custom of the time. It did not necesarily imply lack of care, though it may be deemed irresponsible. I did not feel unloved or unwanted; I accepted my life as perfectly predictable and ordinary. There was a genuine bond of affection with almost every one of the women who had been hired to look after me, yet it was not a surrogate, as far as I can tell, for parental love. Though in early childhood I saw my parents much less frequently than Australian children see (or used to see) at least their mothers, my memories of my early years are on the whole pleasant—family picnics, summer holidays at a mountain resort (accompanied, it is true, by a retinue consisting of maid and nanny) and various outings to the city which always came to an end in a gilded café filled with mouth-watering delicacies.

I recall only one episode of brutality, and that had a swift and significantly predictable consequence. I was scared of moths and beetles (and still detest them when they fly into our bedroom on summer nights). One of my German nannies decided that this childish fear had to be cured. I remember being carried into my room after my bath; I remember the white sheet on the bed; I remember black beetles crawling over the snowy sheet; I remember the crunch of those carapaces as I was lowered into bed; I remember screaming in terror; and I remember that this particular nanny had disappeared by morning. My parents were outraged by her gratuitous cruelty. They were also dismayed, I think, at what they saw as their own irresponsibility. Though the allure of the good life was strong—perhaps too strong—they saw clearly what their responsibilites were, and those responsibilities were fundamentally indistinguishable from the standards of my paternal grandmother's bourgeois dedication to the family and the clan.

The war and, later, life in Australia were to confirm the strength of those responsibilities, decencies and obligations. My parents, but especially my mother, the flightier and the more romantic of the two, rose splendidly to the demands of a harsh life. Those charmed years when money was plentiful, when the menace of the great world seemed very far away from the comfortable safety of Budapest, were in truth no more than a sport, a vacation from their essentially conventional and family-oriented view of the world. Their difficult and in many ways dreary life in Australia was in essence no different from the difficult and dreary life their parents often had to endure. The dismalness of Hurlstone Park or Epping was no worse than the dullness of that plebeian quarter of Budapest which my father's family considered home. Life in Sydney was harder but in essence no different from the life into which they were born. It was only that its details—I am tempted to call them accidentals—the stage-setting for their difficulties were very different. And there had been those golden years, which a brutal and horrible war swept away relentlessly. Those could not be easily forgotten.

As the years passed, my mother came increasingly to think about Sopron, its cosy compactness, and that curious vision of a cultivated life passed on to her by the Ursuline ladies. My father, in his turn, remembered more and more details of his life in my grandmother's stuffy, overfurnished flat. He recalled the family gatherings on cold winter days around the great tile stove. Quite insignificant memories of family life—like the provincial cousin who arrived one day large with child claiming a safe haven, only to withdraw, a day or two later, the cushion she had hidden under her dress—began to assume great importance for him. This was partly a result of the process of ageing. But it was more than that. For both of my parents, in their different ways, these memories represented, despite my mother's recollections of the terror of 1919, a time of peace and stability and of an ordered society—the old world before the flood swept it away. By contrast, their golden years, that hectic time of metropolitan smartness and fast living—though sorely missed—was, they realised, the first warning of that inundation. In one of the last conversations I had with my father, a day or two before his sudden death, he acknowledged that all that nightclubbing, the high life of the late thirties, was nothing other than an attempt to keep fear down, or at least to drown it in some good wine.

AFTER
THE
FALL

Persecution, war and famine are classic themes in the literature of migration. My parents and I experienced all three, but we were fortunate: we survived. The hardships and brutalities we suffered—in common with millions of others from one end of Europe to the other—provided the impetus for our leaving the old world to seek safety in the new. Yet in our case at least, these experiences played a smaller part in the evolution of our ambivalent relationship with our new home than memories of the past or fantasies about the future. It would serve little purpose to recount the tale of our survival, or to tell how we were reunited in a devastated Budapest in the spring of 1945. Though that time left scars on each of us, they soon disappeared from our conscious minds, leaving behind merely traces of fear and anxiety. To this day I feel uneasy when I hear a distant siren in the still of the night or see a searchlight in a festive sky. I do not, however, recall ever having been tortured in my dreams by recognisable icons of persecution and brutality. In all probability, the effect of those years on people like me is deeply ingrained within our personalities; but they are of much less significance to the web of social and cultural interactions I am uncovering in these pages.

In Australia my parents were always reluctant to speak about the worst of their wartime experiences. This may have been due to a natural reticence on their part, or perhaps it was because, compared with the atrocities so many people had suffered, we had got off relatively lightly. I know that they found distasteful—as I still find distasteful—the way some people exploited the events of that time for purposes which were not far removed from emotional blackmail. Making those more fortunate than you uncomfortably aware of their advantages may become a powerful means of imposing your will on them, even of exercising power over them. Such a desire for domination may take the shape of a licensed and at times outrageous eccentricity, as Patrick White showed with his extraordinary recreation of the archetypal survivor, Lotte Lippmann, in *The Eye of the Storm*. It may also manifest itself through a constant insistence that, because of such apocalyptic experiences, the survivor's sensibility and sensitivity are somehow sharper, more perceptive, and therefore worthy of special attention and respect. In the mid-sixties, a middle-aged Viennese lady effectively disrupted a course on twentieth-century literature I was teaching by leaping to her feet at every opportunity to roll back her sleeve and display the number tattooed on her arm. 'What do you know about *The Waste Land*?' she would screech at a roomful of embarrassed young people. 'You know nothink until you know zis!'

For us, and I suspect that this holds true for most other migrants, the months (for some people years) we spent in 1946 in a state of anticipation, waiting to begin our journey to Australia, a land that would ensure safety and happiness, provided by far the most important influences in our efforts to understand and to come to terms with our new home. In my own case, that period, extending from the last months of 1945 until the late November of 1946, determined much more of my life than I could have realised at the time. It provided our last experiences of the old world, even though that world had been almost obliterated or altered beyond recognition. It formed the perspective from which we viewed both the past and, after our arrival in Sydney, what the future might be. That time was a node, an intersection, a crossing of the ways which influenced different people in different ways. For me, at the impressionable age often its effect was to be like those drugs that are designed to dissolve slowly in order to suppress the symptoms of flu or hay fever over a lengthy period. It is only now, after having retraced my steps to the past, that I am able to see with any clarity how much of my personality, longings, desires, and how many of my prejudices and *idées fixes* stem from those strange months of hectic activity and aimless anticipation.

The setting for those feverish months was not the villa of my earliest memories but a three-room flat in the centre of Budapest. We had moved there in 1942, or perhaps early in 1943, because the location of that house in the 'country', formerly the source of great pride for my parents, turned out to be one of the first districts in and around Budapest to attract the attention of Allied bombers. It was not far from a small airfield which, as Hungary came to be more and more involved in a war that until then had been relatively far away and therefore unmenacing, provided a base for the Stukas, Heinkels and Messerschmitts of the Luftwaffe. Consequently, we were obliged to spend more and more time in our neighbours' cellar—our 'ultra-modern' villa had no such amenity—listening for an unmistakable whine indicating that a bomb was about to hit the ground. After several weeks of ever-increasing air-raids my parents decided to seek a safer place to live.

It took time, of course, to find something suitable. Meanwhile we were obliged to accept subterranean hospitality from our neighbours, who had been good friends and partici-pants in my parents' nightclubbing in happier times. Now, however, unspoken but very real tensions began to appear. My parents came to experience a disturbing and paradoxical state of mind that was to come to a climax in the last months of 1944, when Budapest was subjected to almost incessant carpet-bombing. The terrors of civilians subjected to such air-raids requires no comment; the psychological condition of those victims who see these instruments of destruction as their means of liberation should provide, I think, vitally interesting data for the annals of psychopathology. Such was not the case with our neighbours, Croatians (though the wife, who was born in Trieste, claimed to be Italian) and fervent supporters of the Axis powers—though after the war they insisted, of course, that they had never agreed with the racial policies of those régimes.

At length a flat was found in a newly constructed block— probably the last to be built in Budapest for many years— in a quiet residential street near a large park, well away from any military installation, or so my parents imagined. They turned out to have been as mistaken in this belief as in so much else; they had not reckoned with the innocent-looking church on the edge of the park at the top of the street, the crypt of which had been turned into a massive arsenal. That part of the city sustained some of the most concentrated bombing-raids of the last months of the war, when waves of American bombers literally blacked out large areas of the sky above. Miraculously, though, the building itself escaped all but minor damage.

The smell of damp cement, of drying plaster, and of green timber hastily painted or polished are my most haunting memories of the flurry of activity that accompanied our preparations to occupy the apartment. There was need for haste; every day's delay meant more raids against the airfield, more nights spent in our neighbours' cellar crouching on straw mattresses. But certain proprieties had to be observed before the flat was deemed ready for occupation. For one thing, new furniture had to be obtained, for the large art-deco pieces in fiercely patterned walnut which had been especially made for the villa would clearly not do. It was unthinkable for people like my parents to buy ready-made furniture in a shop. New pieces had to be ordered from trusted craftsmen, care had to be exercised over the choice of fabrics to match the texture of the walls, which were not painted but sprayed with a gun to produce a stippled effect—the ultimate in chic. All this took considerable time. We were waiting for furniture that would last a lifetime. Meanwhile the bombing raids against the airfield increased in ferocity. My parents did not ask themselves, it seems to me, how long a lifetime might be.

Finally everything was ready. We moved in. Preparations were made for a housewarming party held behind blackout screens and accompanied by the distant thudding of an air-raid, perhaps on that hapless airfield. The record player and the green-eyed radio, which had come with us, blared out whatever tunes were the hits of the day. Putting the radio in the living room represented a considerable risk. It should have had a device fitted to it to make it incapable of receiving the world services of the BBC. It lived for most of the time in a broom cupboard under piles of blankets. My parents would shut themselves in that cupboard to listen to 'real' news, even though they risked terrible penalties if they were caught. The extension cord trailing from the cupboard to a power point in the entrance hall of the flat was a dead giveaway; but at least the piles of blankets muffled the sound of the radio from the ears of the ever-vigilant caretaker.

He was a revered figure of tyrannical power and authority. He supervised not merely the orderly conduct of the building—making sure that rubbish was disposed of in the required manner, that children did not make too much noise in the stairwell, that the glass panels in the front door of each apartment were cleaned properly—but also the political inclinations of his tenants. Like all such functionaries he was believed to be a police-informer—which he no doubt was. He was not, however, entirely incorruptible. A sufficiently large 'tip' ensured that he allowed the noise level of my parents' housewarming party to exceed what may be termed, I suppose, the level for which no charge was levied. But he could not be trusted, no matter how large the bribe, with the secret of the undoctored radio. On the night of the party it was not produced until all the guests had arrived, and a cloth to be thrown over it was ready to meet the eventuality of an unexpected caller.

I searched for that block of flats on Christmas Eve in 1990. I knew the name of the street but I had forgotten or was confused about the number. As I walked down that drab thoroughfare lined by blackened, crumbling buildings on each side, stucco peeling from their pompous neo-baroque façades to reveal layers of crudely made bricks, nothing spoke to me of familiarity, nothing gave me the sense that I had been there before, or that this was somehow a part of my life. I could have been strolling through a giant postmodernist stage set. Gradually and disturbingly, though, I became aware of a trickle of recognition. The past was returning. The clatter of a distant tram; a grandiose, now disintegrating mythological personage, arms crossed above his head to support the balcony over the gateway of a building; the shallow steps leading to a group of shops in a half-basement; the vista of the grimy street itself; and above all, something in the air, in the atmosphere (a sort of genius of the place) all gave this particular street a unique and individual presence, despite the fact this street scene was mirrored by many other streets of the city, indeed by countless streets the world over— without, it is true, the quantity of dirt and pollution I found around me.

Suddenly, I saw the building. There was no need to look at the street-number, 31B, to discover whether that stirred any memories. Nor was there any need to search the façade to find our balcony or the window of my room. It gave me a momentary shock to realise that the glass in that window was unmarked. Memory prompted me to expect to see the neat round hole, surrounded by a symmetrical web of craze-lines, the result of a shot fired one night by a revelling Russian soldier. I had forgotten the incident, just as I had forgotten how my horrified parents extracted the bullet from the wall beside my bed, and made me sleep thereafter in the unused maid's room that gave onto a gloomy light-well. It was an odd, unsettling moment. The past and present were beginning to merge. Their images were in the process of being super-imposed to form a satisfying whole, in the way that several coloured plates are printed over a sheet of paper to produce a glowing, richly-hued image.

That moment of recovery and reintegration, when I was coming into contact with a past that had been largely for-gotten, or had lain dormant in my memory, was destroyed as I began to look at the building itself. In place of that shipshape construction smelling of newly-laid cement, kept in order by a feared caretaker, there stood a mean, decaying pile, its blackened walls streaked with evil-looking vertical stripes the colour of rust, or perhaps of dried blood. Its balconies, especially our balcony, were sagging perilously, their iron balustrades twisted and, here and there, displaying dangerous gaps. The glass panels in the wings of the entrance door were opaque with dirt. Through the gap I could see—and smell—a Dalek-like garbage container which should have been emptied, judging by the stink, weeks ago. A dog-eared piece of paper fastened to the wall beside the entrance gave the list of tenants and adumbrated the rules governing the conduct of the building. It was signed with the name of the 'Leader of the Tenants' Co-operative'. I stood in front of the doorway. My son took a photograph. When the film was developed I saw myself grimacing at the camera.

Later that day, back at the hotel, surrounded by acres of plywood and plastic, I tried to come to terms with the sense of disappointment and anticlimax this encounter had pro-duced, a feeling not unlike the flatness that overcame my parents and me, all those years before, when the *Marine Phoenix* sailed past the row of streetlights near South Head. I reminded myself that forty-four years had passed since I last stood in that doorway, that those years were bound to have taken their toll on even the most lovingly cherished of buildings, let alone one that had seen war, revolution, and neglect bred out of apathy and indigence. And besides, I also had to remind myself, those forty-four years had not left me entirely untouched.

Such calming thoughts—telling you to be grown-up and sensible, and not to allow your emotions to run away with you—were followed by the recognition of another, perhaps even more disturbing possibility. Could it be that the building, indeed the whole city, had always been like this? After all, I had spent almost half a century amidst Australian standards of hygiene, in a world where even the dunny-men of Epping displayed a certain fastidiousness as they ran along a moonlit driveway. Perhaps this world, the memory of which had been preserved for me by a lovingly nurtured mythology, had always been as grimy, decrepit, ill-organised and foul-smelling as that building, that street, indeed as all of Budapest in those dank, pollution-choked days before Christmas during which I had tried to recapture the past. Was the golden world lamented in countless espresso-bars in Sydney and London, and no doubt in Melbourne, Toronto and Buenos Aires, in reality no more than a shabby aggregation of ill-kept buildings? Had Budapest always been essentially of the Third World? Had those of us who had retained a glowing memory of this world been perpetuating a lie for so many years? I could not find then, as I cannot find now, an answer to these riddles. Perhaps no-one can.

That block of flats, where I spent only a few months of my life, provided the setting from which I observed, with the growing perceptiveness of a ten-year-old old before his time, the febrile world of postwar Budapest, a world which was to persist until the time of our departure for Australia, and indeed for some months beyond that. The memory of that time, which has faded in one sense but has gained in intensity in another, was to colour our attitudes to life in Australia for many years. Many of the problems and perplexities we experienced during our first years in this country grew out of the atmosphere of those hectic months in Budapest, as much as out of the real or imagined hostility and strangeness of our new environment.

We lived in that flat in Budapest until the end of 1944. We returned to it after the city had been liberated, regaining, from families that had camped there during the height of the siege, occupation of at first one, then two and at length every room. It was there that my mother nursed my seriously wounded father, with whom we had been reunited early in 1945 in circumstances so extraordinary that recounting them would offend against credibility. She saved his life, but she could not have accomplished that feat without the kindness of one of the tenants in the building, a recently widowed woman who had turned her flat into a brothel for officers of the occupying forces. This supplied her with food and fuel, which she generously shared with us, and also put her in touch with a source of otherwise unobtainable drugs that were needed to prevent my father's infected wounds from festering. It was in that flat, in a remarkably short time (after, incidentally, the widow had closed the doors of her brothel and returned to her former respectability), that the old patterns of life reasserted themselves, though in a significantly feverish and hectic manner.

The flavour of that time is best described as an uneasy mixture of frantic activity and aimlessness. Though the city had not been as seriously damaged as Dresden or even Vienna, when the Germans and their Hungarian henchmen were finally defeated in the early spring of 1945, much of it lay in ruins. Life contracted into small spaces: people huddling around a feeble brazier (if they were lucky), or merely huddling together. The long nights were illuminated by a shoelace or a piece of string burning in a jar lid filled with rancid oil. There was little food, mostly tins of bully beef of dubious quality and even more uncertain state of preservation. You could, at first, obtain meat of sorts from the bloated carcasses of horses which lay scattered all over the city, but my mother could not bring herself to join the queues of people waiting with hastily sharpened knives to take their cut.

Recovery was, nevertheless, swift. This probably came about through that resilience and inventiveness of the Hungarian character which has spawned several wry jokes, like the one about a Hungarian entering a revolving door behind you and coming out in front. The city picked itself up and dusted its clothes with aplomb. Though there were bomb-sites and craters everywhere, though the supply of gas, electricity and water was erratic and unreliable, though the sweet smell of decomposing flesh hung over the piles of rubble and the mass graves dug in the municipal gardens (strenuously denied by the authorities, but known to everyone), Budapest enjoyed—if that is the word—the benefits of a free-enterprise society with verve and gusto. The communist takeover a few months after we left put a clamp on this activity for many years to come—until indeed a few months before my return at Christmastime in 1990, when once more the city was witnessing scenes not unlike those that characterised the heady days of 1945 and 1946. Then, everyone had something to sell. Everyone found some way of participating in the complicated economic networks that had sprung up everywhere like toadstools.

The result was chaos; but it was chaos of a wonderfully exhilarating sort. The whole city was on the move. People hurried about with whatever commodity they possessed to strike deals with owners of other commodities. They rushed along the crowded pavements, neatly sidestepping piles of rubble or gaping holes, or else were carried about in an astonishing variety of horse-drawn vehicles—clapped-out fiacres, hansom-cabs, aristocratic landaus, barouches and cabriolets, their pompous crests still faintly visible on their faded and crazed coachwork. No-one was empty-handed. You carried whatever you intended to sell, or whatever you had just purchased—bolts of cloth, ancient eiderdowns, the horn of an old-fashioned gramophone, pots of glue and paint, shoe-trees, stethoscopes. Anything and everything had value. Someone somewhere would find a use for any object, no matter how bizarre or broken-down. People were thirsty for success, for the accumulation of wealth out of whatever they had rescued from the ruin of their lives, and they lusted after the outward and visible emblems of wealth. In the crowded cafés everyone boasted of his good fortune while keeping a weather-eye open for the main chance.

All this was, it goes without saying, a perilous and unhealthy world which would have collapsed of its own energy, greed and lawlessness even if the grim-faced comrades hadn't quashed it with a ham-fisted blow. Money had become worthless. One stifling day my mother and I set out for the nearby baths. One bag contained our swimming gear, the other was stuffed full of banknotes. We stood in the queue at the ticket booth amid the throng of people seeking relief from the heatwave. We had almost reached the top of the line when an official emerged and rubbed out the admission price chalked on a blackboard beside the booth, substituting a figure a few millions greater. We didn't have enough. When we got back to the flat, we dragged a suitcase from the broom cupboard which had formerly housed the clandestine radio, and stuffed several million more into our moneybag. But it was to no avail—by the time we reached the ticket booth once more, the price had gone up again.

You only used money for things like tram tickets. After a while the conductors refused to collect fares, overburdened as they were by satchels containing sums of money which could only be represented by figures, not by words. Currency could not buy real goods or services. The economy subsisted on barter (which was tolerated) or on American dollars or, better still, gold coins, chiefly louis d'or and the occasional English sovereign (both dollars and coins wholly illegal, with frightful penalties for those caught in possession). Where formerly we lived in dread of inspectors seeking to sniff out the least trace of political unreliability or a radio capable of receiving the BBC, our hearts now missed a beat every time the doorbell rang, wondering whether it was the inspector (often the same person as before) in search of illicit currency.

People expended extraordinary ingenuity in contriving safe hiding places for their hoards. Rumour spread its net around neighbourhoods and communities. Never in the spines of books! They arrested someone at Number 47 last week. My parents thought they had been very clever when they worked out how to loosen the lead seal on the electricity meter, thus enabling the cover to be lifted and the cavity behind it to be stuffed with banknotes and coins. Then we heard that Mrs Somebody had been dragged off by the police when they discovered a roll of American dollars in her meter. We tried the lining of topcoats; we tried the back of the green-eyed radio; my mother had the wedge heels of her summer sandals hollowed. Our precious dollars and gold coins led a restless life, constantly moving about the flat, our clothes and our possessions in search of safety. We were always on the lookout, always alert and watchful, apprehensive, forever trying to anticipate whatever 'their' next move might be.

It was a neurotic world, bordering on hysteria. A curious excitement filled the air, a recklessness with a touch of hectic gallantry. People were living their lives to the full, as if there were no future. For some there was none. For some there was only ruin—financial, political and physical. For others, like my parents, the future was the peaceful dullness of places like Epping. But even for them that peace soon turned to ashes through economic hardship and the boredom of living in a world entirely lacking the excitement of their last months in the old world.

Like most other children living through those strange days, I fell under the spell of that carnival of excess, anxiety and excitement. Like my parents, like everyone else, I was in a state of anticipation, of marking time, and while I was marking time, I engaged with the pleasures of life—at least as far as they were available to me. For the first time in my life, apart from a couple of weeks spent at a nursery school some years earlier, I was to attend school. My education was, however, shortlived. On my second day, a barber came into the classroom carrying the sinister appurtenances of his trade:

razor, brush, bowl and strop. We—thirty or forty squirming boys—had to submit to the indignity of having our heads shaved as a precaution against lice. My parents were outraged. They took me out of school—we would after all be leaving for Australia soon. Officialdom ignored my truancy. My schooling was not to begin until I was past my eleventh birthday, when I was received into the perplexed bosom of Canterbury Public School in New South Wales.

The months of aimless activity that followed my two days of schooling provide my most significant memories of that former life, a life that abruptly ceased to exist as soon as we caught sight of those streetlights near South Head the following year. Much of that time I spent in the company of my maternal grandmother, who had grown even more sour and mean-spirited in that hectic and self-indulgent world. No doubt we did all sorts of things which I have now forgotten; some of my most powerful and evocative memories of that time are concerned with our frequent visits to a funfair. That funfair, modelled (like so much else in Budapest) on the famous, and much larger, Prater in Vienna, stood—and still stands—in the public gardens which began at the top of our street. My grandmother and I would stroll in a leisurely fashion towards its gateway, and enter a magical world.

It boasted the usual attractions of such places, but my grandmother and I spent an eternity—or so memory tells me—visiting two of them in particular. One was called Venice, a kitschy version of the Tunnel of Love. To the accompaniment of a cracked, hissing recording of the Barcarolle from *The Tales of Hoffmann*, your gondola glided down the dark waters of the Grand Canal, past imposing palaces, past the magical façade of a cardboard Ca' d'Oro, under a rickety Rialto, until, as a *pièce de résistance* just before the conclusion of this dreamlike tour on the other side of a canvas flap, the Piazetta, with the noble domes of San Marco and an admittedly foreshortened Campanile, floated into view. The enchantment of gliding down those black waters, surrounded by the magic of the Venetian night, was almost unbearable.

My grandmother always sat impassively beside me, wearing her heavy topcoat, into the lining of which our golden wealth had been carefully sewn.

The other attraction, the Midget Theatre, could have stepped straight out of one of Fellini's improbable fantasies. We sat on folding chairs under a striped tent in front of a makeshift stage on which a company of midgets performed a repertoire of sketches and short plays. I can remember nothing about their plots or subject matter, or any of the dialogue which, I suspect, may have been quite obscene. All that remains with me is a handful of images. I remember one of the players in an elaborate wedding gown, so made as to exaggerate the shortness of her stature and the disproportionate size of her head. She clutched a wilted bouquet almost as large as herself. She was weeping disconsolately while recounting an endless tale of woe—no doubt about the lover who had jilted her at the altar. Another image has even less context: two personages in morning dress—grey toppers and silver-knobbed canes—probably drunk, arguing about something. I remember several musical numbers including two policemen singing 'The Gendarmes' Duet'. But best of all was the grand finale of many of these shows, a group of midgets in full habit marching onto the stage to the accompaniment of the angelus bell singing something vaguely religious, probably 'The Nuns' Chorus'.

Those days spent at the funfair seem in retrospect emblematic of the folly and pathos of that strange time. Many of us lived in a world of illusions, a world where the shabby imitation—whether a cut-out Venice or those unfortunate stunted creatures aping the lives of 'big' people—was preferable and considered superior to the real and the substantial. Our sensibilities had, somehow, been thrown out of kilter. We turned our back on the world of everyday reality in favour of a carefully stage-managed dream in which the cheaply romantic rubbed shoulders with the grotesque. When, amidst the paspalum of Epping, I, like my parents, began to yearn for Europe, I did not dream of my father's solidly bourgeois world, nor about the cosiness of my mother's home town, nor even about my few memories of golden summers in our villa, but of the ecstasy and enchantment generated by paint, canvas and paste. The past had become indistinguishable from the wonders of another astonishing theatrical illusion, one for which Venice and the Midget Theatre were no more than a preparation. My memories of the romance of Europe, cherished and worshipped under the harsh Australian sunshine, amidst the anguish and discontents of adolescence in a strange land, came to focus on the most curious and memorable of my experiences of the last months of our life in the old world, something far excelling the many enchantments of the funfair.

A NIGHT
AT THE
OPERA

During that year in which I spent many of my daylight hours in Venice or at the Midget Theatre, when the smell of death still hung over the city, as bodies continued to be extracted from the rubble, and as the occasional blast of a buried bomb shook the few windowpanes that remained, the Budapest Opera House opened its doors. The building was a blaze of light in a darkened city. Whole districts had their uncertain supply of low-voltage electricity cut off to illuminate the marble foyers, gilt auditorium and spacious stage of an elaborately over-embellished theatre. The treacherous allure of Venice and of the Midget Theatre was enacted on a gigantic scale as the whole population, it seemed, flocked to marvel once more at painted vistas of grandeur and romance, and to fall under the spell of the arm-flailing passions of love, lust, revenge, hate, treachery, nobility and despair. The tragic fortunes of noble courtesans and jilted queens, of cruel tyrants and traduced princes, seemed more real, and were certainly charged with far deeper significance, than the reminders of the real-life apocalypse visible in the world outside the resplendent theatre.

The Central European mania for opera—incomprehensible to the Anglo-Saxon sensibility—reached its apotheosis in that wanton squandering of scarce resources on a form of entertainment that many would regard as the most mindlessly

71

self-indulgent and bombastic of the arts. It is difficult for those who were not brought up within this deeply ingrained habit or tradition to appreciate the profound social, cultural and perhaps even spiritual significance of opera for the people of Central Europe. For them opera is much more than, at best, a powerful form of musical theatre or, at worst, an inane farrago of tortured plots and turgid music. It is, on the contrary, a way of life, a symbol of aspirations tinged, at times, with near-religious import. It provides the basis for a social ritual in which music and performance are merely important parts of a much larger whole. Opera is one of the means—perhaps the crucial one—of such a society's celebrating itself as a superior civilisation. For that reason, in Budapest, as in those cities where the opera houses escaped total destruction, performances began to be held while the city still bore fresh signs of war and carnage, when there were many shortages and privations, when there was considerable danger attached to the simple act of going to the opera and returning home after the performance.

As you walked past mountains of rubble, you were confronted by all manner of perils. You had to be careful not to lose your footing, especially if you had forgotten to bring a torch. There was always the danger that a loose bit of masonry would come crashing down from a damaged building. Sinister shapes would sometimes leap out of the shadows. Local vagabonds, half-starved and often half-crazed, were not too difficult to discourage; not so drunk Russian soldiers, out for a bit of innocent fun. Nevertheless people flocked enthusiastically to the opera.

Only a great deal of string-pulling and the distribution of substantial bribes permitted my parents not merely to obtain a subscription but to regain the box they had occupied on Wednesday nights until air-raids and the siege obliged the theatre to close. Throughout that year, as they were cutting one by one their ties with the old life, their attention turned very much to last things: we would all go to the opera for one last season. There was no doubt in their minds that their new home would offer a theatre and an ambience as splendid as this had been, but they were fond of the old place; they thought it well worth the bother of picking our way laboriously home after each performance. And, in any event, it would be nice for me to remember what our Opera House had been like. So, on almost every Wednesday night throughout that year, with only a brief remission during high summer, we went to the opera to witness tales of lust and passion. Those magical nights were my initiation into a world of fabulous wonder which dazzled my eyes more than it enchanted my ears. I entered a dream world which has never lost its allure for me.

I must not give an impression of a phenomenally precocious child savouring the nuances of a complex and demanding art form. I was not entirely unfamiliar with opera, for there were recordings of operatic extracts among my parents' collection of popular songs and dance music. Nevertheless, the enchantment of opera was only partly, perhaps not even predominantly, musical. A performance of *Tristan and Isolde* conducted by the great Klemperer left me unmoved and, by the end, bored beyond endurance. I would give anything now to hear that performance again. The allure of opera was for me visual and atmospheric; music was no more than an accompaniment to the romantic experience that engulfed me as the houselights dimmed and the first sounds emerged from the orchestra pit.

Our box was in the lowest tier, just above the level of the stalls, a little too far to the side but still among the most desirable locations according to the strictly codified hierarchy that governed the construction of such theatres. Its four gilt-and-plush chairs were complemented by a high stool with a small back support and a raised footrest; it allowed a view of the stage over the heads of the other occupants. An anteroom contained a mirror, several coat-hooks (for the proud possession of a box relieved the necessity of having to mingle with the *canaille* at the cloakroom), and a chaise-longue, the function of which was not at all clear to me at the time.

The anteroom could be separated from the box by a plush curtain, an offspring perhaps of the great braided curtain hanging over the stage.

If you leaned on the padded balustrade at the front of the box, which was ample enough to allow opera glasses and ladies' purses to rest on it without the danger of their tumbling over, the social world spread out in front of you could be surveyed with all the elaboration of an arcane ritual. Admittedly, what you saw in 1946 were row upon row of bemedalled Russian officers, stiffly signifying their respect for culture. Yet on those Wednesday nights my mother's eyes, mouth and hands nevertheless performed a complicated dance of recognition, greeting, surprise, mild censure for some sartorial *faux pas*—in short that vocabulary of signs unique to the culture of Central European opera audiences, which were so ingrained in people like her that they would not yield even in the face of the harshest reality. Most of the people who had engaged in this strange ritual with her in earlier years were dead. But her eyes and hands continued to move in an instinctive, indeed involuntary manner.

The rising of the curtain transported me into another world. Those were still the days of fussily realistic scenery—most of it predating the war—and visual tricks which, to my eyes, defied belief. Venusberg, with its twisted limestone pillars and massive outcrops, was transformed within an instant into a pleasant valley bathed in morning light. The great ramparts of the Wartburg were clearly visible in the distance; the shepherd-lad playing sweetly on his pipe was seated on a grassy knoll carpeted with flowers. The story of Tosca's doomed love for the painter Cavaradossi reached its climax under the huge bulk of the Castel Sant' Angelo; once again you could hear a shepherd greeting the dawn. The great dome of St Peter's rose out of the mist, but a few stars still twinkled in the sky above to allow the painter to sing the song we all knew. There were terrors as well. Dr Miracle's sinister shape, as he tempted the hapless Antonia to sing, and thus hasten her death, multiplied itself, scattering its reflection into every nook and cranny of the stage, from which he leered at the dying invalid. Mephistopheles hovered above the grieving Marguerite, mocking the chains that bound her to her dark prison. As the statue of the Commendatore strode into the vast hall where Don Giovanni supped alone, I experienced a shudder almost as violent as that which shook the manservant cowering near the footlights.

This dream world was not the happiest or the healthiest of influences. Its glamour was too enticing for anyone—let alone an impressionable child—living in a shattered city which had come close to destruction. Though what I saw on stage almost always dealt with suffering, disaster, treachery and death, these afflictions were endured with dignity and sonorous heroism. Dying sopranos forgave their errant lovers with sweetly melodious nobility. Villainous baritones went to their deaths with spirited defiance, always ending on a ringing note that brought the house down. The betrayed king raised his hands in benediction over the bodies of his wife and her lover, the nephew who had been like a son to him. Here was a world, in short, where the horrors and miseries of our life—the signs of which were still visible as we left the theatre huddled in groups for greater safety—were transformed into beauty and nobility.

I was not the first to discover consolation in art. But the consolation opera offered at that time was spurious and unhealthy. It led me into a world of showy glamour where romantic images and the warm sonority of the music—though I suspect that most of the performances were second-rate—acted as powerful drugs and distractions. Because we lived in such a feverish, hectic and provisional world, because we were waiting to enter into a state of permanence and normality, the sensuous images of opera came, quite insidiously, to represent the normality we were anticipating. Perhaps I should not admit it, but ever since those days a part of my imagination has whispered to me (despite the mockery of my rational self) that somewhere in the world there might exist a place where a forlorn maiden stands beside a moonlit tower, listening to her lover's heartrending song, while, in the distance, the solemn chant of monks declares that the hour of his death is near. My wife and sons often remind me that whenever I arrive in a European city, the first thing I do is to find out what is on at the opera.

We lamented the absence of opera during our early years in Sydney. Needless to say, the regret was purely hypothetical. Had we found that superb theatre among swaying palms, we would not have been able to afford the price of admission. But the longing was, of course, deeply symbolic. The opera, with its brilliant lights and its elegant audience murmuring politely before the curtain rose, became an emblem for a lost paradise—one we had already lost when we sat in our box surveying the rows of bull-necked Russians spread out before us. And consequently I have been searching for that paradise ever since. A few years after we arrived in Sydney my father took me to the gods of the old Theatre Royal, or perhaps of the more plebeian Tivoli, to hear a performance of *Tosca* by a touring Italian company. I later learnt that some of the performers we heard that night were among the best stock-singers of the time—certainly not the luminaries of the international festival circuit, but probably far superior to the war-wearied hacks Budapest was able to muster in 1946. My response was, nevertheless, one of bitter disappointment. Where were the massive walls of the fortress? Where was the dome of the basilica, or the twinkling in the sky? A shaking canvas flat with a few clumsy brush-strokes to represent huge granite blocks was no substitute for the reality—far more real than anything else in my experience—which I had seen come to life on the vast, noble stage of *our* Opera House.

I have visited, since that time, many of the world's great opera houses, and have heard singers who have already become legendary. I have been present when Schwarzkopf made everyone's heart break at the end of the first act of *Der Rosenkavalier*.

I witnessed the young Sutherland's triumph as Lucia. I have heard Nilsson and Windgassen burning with passion in the second act of *Tristan and Isolde*, and the great Hans Hotter in one of his last appearances as Wotan. I fell under the sweet spell of de los Angeles as the dying Mimi. I have heard some of the world's most renowned operatic conductors, and seen the work of many brilliant directors and designers. Yet on none of those occasions, whether in London, Milan, Vienna or Bayreuth, was I able to recapture the excitement of those nights at the opera when, as a wide-eyed child, I was seized by the enchantment of dangerous illusions and treacherous conjuring tricks. Perhaps only a child may experience such things. Nevertheless memories of that state of ecstatic trance into which I fell on most of those nights are inseparable from the fact that they were lost when we embarked on our attempt to establish a new life under different skies. It is an experience I am still searching—in vain, I know—to recapture.

When I returned to Budapest after that long absence, I anticipated my usual habits by arriving armed with a ticket to the opera. I had arranged in Vienna, where tickets for the Budapest opera are obtainable for next-to-nothing in order to provide a source of hard currency for Hungary's fledgling free market economy, to attend a performance of *Tannhäuser* on the night after my arrival. At first, the Budapest of 1990 bore little resemblance to the city I had left all those years ago. There were no bomb-sites or craters; trams and buses ran efficiently and taxis were plentiful; the supply of electricity was strong and constant. True, it was a drab and dirty city under a gloomy winter sky. If you looked hard enough you could discover bullet-holes on the façades of many buildings. The smells wafting out of various apertures in the streets did not inspire confidence in the sewerage system. It was all a far cry from the glitz of a Vienna enamoured of its affluence, its shops bursting with Christmas luxuries, its citizens, clad in smart loden-cloth and sporting cocky little feathered hats, drinking mulled wine at open-air booths. This, by comparison, was the grimness of the Third World.

Yet, as I discovered again the once familiar places, as the map of the city which had lain buried in my memory all those years rose once more to the surface of my consciousness, I began to recognise something not at all unlike the excitement of that hectic time in 1946 when the city was beginning to wake from the nightmare of war. This was, after all, the first year of yet another new world for Hungary. The forgetful slumber in which it had languished for almost as long as I had been living in Australia was beginning to pass. Once again, you could see people selling things almost everywhere you looked—'genuine' Russian army hats, statuettes of Lenin (which, no doubt, you could deface at will), embroidered tablecloths ('I need medicine for my blind mother, noble sir'), devotional images, fob-watches with the emblem of the Soviet railways on their lids, enormous flat-irons—anything and everything was for sale in the ferment of a newly-born free market economy. Despite dire warnings posted on the backs of doors in hotel rooms or displayed in cafés and restaurants all over the city, some tourists readily accepted invitations whispered to them in many languages: 'You want exchange? Very good rate!'

In that grimy city, where the superb collection of old masters in the art gallery is disintegrating under the onslaught of damp, mould and neglect, the Opera House stood, as formerly, a resplendent emblem of national pride. The fairy-tale foyers, a late nineteenth-century dream of 'Renaissance' grandeur, the sweep of the auditorium and the graceful proscenium arch were a riot of freshly applied gilt. This was not the faded splendour of theatres like Covent Garden or La Fenice which speak of tradition, of restraint and of the allure of rich but worn magnificence. Here everything was much too bright, raw in its opulence, in the dazzling shine of a newly created world. And when my eyes had adjusted to all that brightness, I realised how small a theatre this was. Where I had remembered a vast auditorium, its tiers of galleries rising to the sky, with an enormous stage capable of containing massive fortresses and vast palaces, I saw a cosy, extravagantly jewelled place, a diminutive, provincial cousin of the great houses in Munich, Dresden and Vienna which it could not match in grandeur but could rival in richness of decoration. A charming place, but not one to inspire awe.

The lights dimmed, the visiting Soviet conductor raised his baton, the first notes of the pilgrims' song rose insecurely from the horns. When, at length, the not very expertly played tumult in the orchestra pit subsided, the curtain went up to reveal a crinkled cyclorama, in front of which a group of young people clad in leotards pranced, leapt up and down and generally rushed around in a fever of activity. Later, Venus' love-nest rose from the depths of the stage, lit by a flickering pink glow and dominated by an enormous plush-covered sofa with large brass studs, on which reclined the Queen of Love. Never was the old joke about the fat lady more to the point. With a flapping double chin and a vibrato a mile wide (the legacy, no doubt, of her Russian training), the singer performed the music efficiently enough. But where was the enchantment, where the glamour? Her dumpy clenched fists and fat little wrists beat time to the music. She shuffled two paces to the right, two paces to the left and collapsed on her sofa as if exhausted from passion and desire, streams of perspiration running down her chubby cheeks.

The performance continued on its pedestrian way. At length the hero escaped from Venusberg and encountered his former friends in the valley of the Wartburg as they were returning from the hunt. Obliging menials trotted around the stage displaying various trophies, principally a reindeer in shiny wax suspended between two poles of machined timber. Meanwhile another drama was brewing in the auditorium. A correctly dressed elderly gentleman began to upbraid a pair of jeans-clad Germans who cuddled and kissed, tickled and slapped (between shared sips from a large bottle of mineral water) in their expensive seats—purchased, no doubt, for a song in Vienna, just as I had purchased mine. Other properly dressed members of the audience, observing this fracas, murmured approbation as the old gentleman's fury rose to heights of vehemence in his defence of the respect to which culture, especially Hungarian culture, should be entitled. I remembered the retired town clerk. I remembered the terrible fuss over my mother's painted fingernails. I grew so discouraged that I left after the second act, going back to my hotel to watch what CNN had to say about the imminent war in the Gulf.

A few days after returning to Sydney I went to the opera again. There was no comparison between the two performances. What I saw and heard at Bennelong Point had the assurance and sophistication of a metropolitan culture. And yet the old worm was already gnawing away inside me. I forgot the fat Venus in her pink suburban disco, the squawks that emerged from the orchestra pit, the clumsy shuffling as the Thuringian nobility arrived to witness the great song contest. What I saw again was that vast, glamorous edifice of my childhood enchantment, an emblem of a marvellously satisfying and romantic world I had lost forever. By comparison, the black shell of the Opera Theatre, its cramped stage, the whole of that brutally practical auditorium spoke of a humdrum and commonplace life. I realised, as I walked out of the theatre into a star-lit summer night, the Harbour twinkling magically with a thousand lights, the open-air cafés serving their last customers, the ferries gliding silently over the mirrored water, that exile seels your eyes, allowing you to see only what your longings and sense of loss will permit.

My mother as the *grande dame* c. 1940. When the Russians
looted our flat in 1945, they put pins through the eyes in
the photograph.

A golden summer in our 'villa', sharing a tub with a cousin.

above
My father in 1942 —
defending the country that,
as it turned out, did not
want to defend him.

left
Photograph taken in 1946
—I think, when I was nine
or ten, but somehow
I seem younger. Could
it be 1942-3, when
I was six or seven?

Arrival in Sydney.

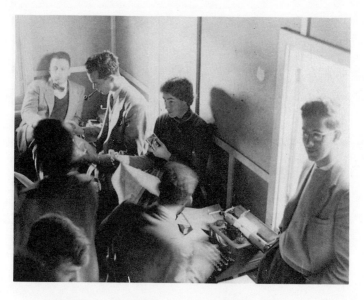

The *Honi Soit* office c. 1957. Robert Hughes is
in the foreground. Also pictured are David Solomon,
Elizabeth Stafford and Martin Davey.

At my 21st birthday party, with, *left to right*: Jan Spratt,
Robert Hughes, Christina Dennis and Jennifer Baume.

On the way to England in 1960, with Jill Kitson on my left. The suntan acquired on the five-week voyage did much to confuse people about my national identity.

Outside the block of flats where we spent our
last months in Budapest.

INSIDE

THE
LANGUAGE
OF THE TRIBE

L anguage holds the key to the newcomer's experience. It
determines the extent to which the migrant may find a
congenial place within his new world. His future—whether
of contentment and a sense of belonging, or of isolation and,
at best, imprisonment within a tightly-knit group— ultimately depends on how efficiently the new language is
acquired. The achievement of that essential feat relies on a
large number of factors, of which age and general linguistic
ability are probably the most important. Some people find
it easier to learn languages than others; the young generally
experience much less difficulty than adults. With adults,
cultural habits and level of education play a most important
role. A well-educated person is more likely to prosper in a
new language than an illiterate, though there are always
exceptions.

For migrants, learning a language implies far more than
the acquisition of a vocabulary and grammar. Some of the
most unfortunate people among my parents' acquaintances
were several cultivated men and women who had an excellent
reading ability in English, representing at times the habit of
a lifetime, who nevertheless could not make the transition
from a basically literary and cultural use of the language to
idiomatic speech. Their precise, clumsy, often excessively
elaborate attempts at spoken English proved an almost

insuperable barrier in those trivial and mundane transactions where linguistic proficiency is tested. At times these people gave offence because there seemed to be something mocking and dismissive in their pompous formality. The truth was, of course, that they were merely using inappropriate tools— they spoke like heavily accented parodies of characters in Dickens because for them writers like Dickens had provided a norm and a model. Their ears were too accustomed to those literary cadences to recognise that what they heard around them each day was in many ways a different language. By contrast, people who learnt English in a haphazard and wholly unsystematic way, as my mother did, were frequently able to communicate freely, because they had a grasp of idiom and had achieved an unconscious recognition of the connection between language and the social reality it conveys. That they spoke in a garbled grammar, or that they never mastered the intricacies of accentuation did not matter very much. Though they always remained quaint, and their speech gave rise at times to amusement, they nevertheless lived within Australian society, even if their position was very close to the margin.

The process of learning a language in such circumstances is essentially indescribable. Once you have learnt what you had not known until then, the former state of ignorance becomes to all intents and purposes incapable of recovery. I am able to remember a time when the meaning of very ordinary English words was unknown to me. I can recall vividly certain occasions when a hitherto meaningless sequence of sounds or letters suddenly acquired sense, when these sounds or letters no longer formed a tantalising puzzle. I can also recall the frustration and disorientation of those early days in Sydney when the sounds we heard around us and the written messages we saw everywhere—shop-signs, newspaper head-lines, advertising hoardings claiming our attention from all sides—were no more than a menacing jumble of insoluble riddles. What I cannot remember at all precisely, though, is the mechanism of that process of learning, nor the point at which the confidently English-speaking child or adolescent finally emerged. The reason for the lack of precise and identifiable memories involves more than the mere passage of time or lapses of memory. It has a great deal to do with the linguistic identity of the individual who is engaged in an attempt to recapture the past.

If I were asked what is my first or native language I would have to say Hungarian, though I am not at all certain that until my fourth or fifth year German would not have had an equal claim. But clearly, my principal language is neither Hungarian nor German, but English. I grew up in English, my adult self is English-speaking and, more importantly, my conceptual and intellectual life exists only within an English-language context. I do not know the Hungarian expressions for countless abstract concepts I use in my everyday life. Nor can I remember the Hungarian words for many commonplace objects. When I lost a glove on a cold winter day in Budapest in 1990, I could not think of the word for glove; a shopkeeper who spoke English had to help me out. I look back on the past therefore from the perspective of English, a language which has shaped my concepts and attitudes. I cannot recapture or convey the experience of learning, of growing familiar with a new language and a new society, because what I was then learning and attempting to absorb is now familiar, it has become an integral part of my self.

In the course of such a process, to learn is also to forget— but not entirely. You can remember events; you may recapture the emotions and the atmosphere of a particular time of your life; humiliations, anxieties and anguish leave indelible marks on your personality. These may be recovered from the past. And there remains, moreover, an ineradicable substratum of your 'native' language ready to pop up like a malicious imp at the least provocation. Yet for me the process of learning inevitably involved the act of unlearning. In my teens I did everything to avoid having to speak Hungarian, assuring my parents' acquaintances that I had forgotten the language. That was, of course, a long way from the truth. Yet Hungarian was in the process of becoming a secondary language. The act of forgetting represented as much a self-willed and symbolic assertion as a natural and inevitable process. This was largely the result of a naive and, it seems to me in retrospect, tiresomely aggressive attempt to become a genuine Australian. It was due in large measure to my inability to reconcile the social, emotional and psychological claims of my two languages.

Hungarian, like most other European tongues, possesses an elaborate system of address which draws subtle distinctions between the familiar and the respectful. Like Italian and German, but unlike French, it uses third-person forms where circumstances demand a polite mode of address. Children may use the second-person to address other children, close members of their family and, perhaps most significantly, servants. All other adults must be addressed obliquely in the third-person. The point at which adults may pass from the third-person to the second is determined by the same conditions that allowed people to be on 'first-name terms' in English-speaking societies before the days of the ubiquitous Christian name. Significantly though, Hungarian permits the use of first names at much earlier stages of a relationship than English does, always with the proviso that such a liberty must be accompanied by the formal or respectful use of third-person forms until a degree of intimacy is achieved. To employ the second-person any earlier would be deeply offensive. A deliberate policy of the Germans and of their Hungarian henchmen during the war was to shout commands in the second-person at groups of people they had rounded up for transportation to Auschwitz, or else to line them up on the banks of the Danube (often where the famous and much-patronised cafés were located) to be sprayed with machine-gun fire. Political and physical brutality inevitably found its mirror in language.

This characteristic of Hungarian is accompanied, moreover, by an elaborate system of social usage which ensures the maintenance of rigid distinctions between the child and the adult, the servant and the master, the powerful and the weak. Well brought up children are expected to address their elders in terms faintly reminiscent of the elaborate ceremonies of the Sun King's court. In my childhood, you were expected to say that you wanted to kiss grown-ups' hands whenever you met them, even though to kiss someone's hand, at least in my parents' circle, would have been considered precocious and offensive. That privilege was reserved for grown men when they met ladies of their acquaintance; it was at times accompanied by the loud clicking of heels.

Children would, in turn, be addressed by adults in the most cloyingly endearing of terms—with liberal use of second-person pronouns and verbs, whereas children were obliged to use the formal third-person mode in their dealings with their elders. Hungarians commonly fawn over children, commenting on and drawing attention to their physical attributes, intelligence, sweetness, the rate of their growth, the condition of their hair and all kinds of other marvels, in much the same way as some Australians and many British people go into ecstasies over household pets. There is something basically shaming and demeaning in these rituals of fawning and petting, as if you were an object rather than a human being. These performances would almost always be addressed to the world at large ('How he's grown, look at his lovely eyes, show me your teeth—what wonderful teeth! and so clever!'). And they would inevitably carry disturbing overtones—the conviction grew on you as these public inspections continued that their direct opposite was intended, that the kind adult thought you were an unbearable brat who should have been drowned at birth.

There was a time when such rituals formed a normal part of my life. You played the game that everybody played. But the laconic games of Australian society threw these practices into an intolerable relief. They may have been very well for a world peopled by his Excellency, the retired town clerk, whose very existence, even in his censorious rages, was governed by a set of highly conventional rules. They were appropriate to a society that had carried the practice of obliqueness and innuendo to the status of a high art. No doubt the relationship between the Ursuline nuns who had taught my mother and those privileged visitors whom they received in their elegant salon was governed by elaborate rules of evasion, by a structure of hypocrisies to which both parties willingly consented. These would not, however, do in a world where the wonderfully impersonal 'you' is employed in all relationships, where the equally non-committal 'Mr', 'Mrs' or 'Miss' replaced all those Uncles and Aunties whose hands you were expected to offer to kiss. The culture of prewar Central Europe could not be transplanted into Australia's much drier, more matter-of-fact soil. I could not therefore reconcile the contrary demands made on my social behaviour. It was much easier to pretend that I had forgotten the language. I had come to realise instinctively what linguists were to teach me in later life: that a society's essence, the rules that govern its conduct, and the aspirations that provide its vital energies all find their subtlest yet most powerful expression in language, that complex instrument for preserving and celebrating a unique way of life.

I had to unlearn or suppress—it comes to much the same thing—our old way of life in my attempt to become assimilated, that is to say, to assume the forms, rituals and habits of a very different culture. I cannot say which direction the primary impulse took: whether the desire to unlearn fuelled my attempts to acquire English, and along with it the social forms it embodied, or whether my eagerness for acceptance by Australian society made the preservation of the old life insupportable. All I know is that the career of a parodist and mimic on which I embarked some little time after our arrival in Australia—a career I have pursued ever since—consisted as much in discarding as in adopting. My past had to be eradicated. I tried to lock away in an inaccessible compartment of my personality the experiences of my last months in Budapest in that spectral world of Venice, the Midget Theatre and the Opera, as well as the years of the war, and the mythology that had accumulated around my family, in short the whole network of influences, emotional and social legacies that define and in a sense create an individual.

The consequences of such major emotional and cultural surgery are, naturally enough, extremely grave. The attempt to remake myself resulted in the many years I spent in an emotional vacuum, or, to find another image, inside a cocoon I had spun around myself until I felt ready to emerge with my new being. But in the way that victims of amputation continue to feel the presence of ghost-like limbs long after they have been removed, so the complex influences which go into the formation of a personality during the early years of life insisted on making their presence felt. Retrospect tells me that during the years of deliberate forgetting and denial—when I went as far as saying to some of my Australian acquaintances that I could remember nothing of the past—those suppressed and despised influences contrived to enter into my emotional life in wholly surprising ways. Initially, though, the more immediate task of learning English had to be addressed.

The beginning of that process was not auspicious. By the autumn of 1947 my parents could no longer justify keeping me away from school. We had been settled in our rented rooms in Hurlstone Park for some weeks, and an attempt had therefore to be made to introduce a measure of normality into what had been a markedly vagrant existence for a child. For the first time, a month or so after my eleventh birthday, I began attending school regularly. I was enrolled at Canterbury Public School, a few minutes' walk from where we lived. My first days there provide some of my most bizarre memories of our early months in Australia.

My appearance in the potholed school playground on a stifling morning in late March caused a sensation. This was due largely to the clothes my mother considered it appropriate for me to wear. In New York, where we spent a few weeks on our way to Australia, she had stocked up at Macy's New Year sale. Her choice of items was probably governed by those Carmen Miranda fantasies that my parents had entertained about life in Australia. On this particular morning she rigged me out for school in a coloured summer shirt, a pair of blue cotton shorts, and brightly-striped socks worn with sandals. The socks, especially, made me the centre of an incredulous circle of onlookers. I was a garish parrot amidst a flock of drab sparrows.

In the late forties Hurlstone Park and Canterbury represented the quintessence of working-class Australia. The rows of mostly single-fronted cottages in the streets of our neighbourhood were separated at the back by rusting sheets of corrugated iron and at the front by flimsy picket fences. At weekends sallow-complexioned men wearing sparklingly clean cotton singlets sat for hours on brown-stained front steps, with bottles of beer perched beside them, addressing the odd laconic remark to their counterparts next door. On weekdays, as they were leaving for the factory or the railway yards where many of them worked, their wives were already out the front, clad in faded dressing-gowns, their heads wrapped in scarves, watering the inevitable hydrangeas that grew beside the steps of most of these houses. Before they had finished watering, their children would be leaving for school, the boys in heavy grey woollen shorts, their hair, like their fathers', brutally 'short-back-and-sides' (as in the terrible indignity suffered by the central character in Patrick White's story 'Clay'), the girls in equally inappropriate blue serge tunics. Girls usually carried Globite schoolcases; the boys considered them too prissy—their books and sandwiches were often conveyed in mustard-coloured shoulder bags which you could buy at disposal stores. My parents never allowed me to have one of those badges of manliness—I had to be content with a sissy Globite.

The bemused boys who surrounded me on that first morning, staring in wonderment at an overcoloured scarecrow, were all lean and sinewy, their faces old for their years, many of them barefooted, their clothes crumpled and dirty. Small eyes looked suspiciously out of freckled faces; thin lips were pursed in disapproval. Even the girls, separated from us by an inviolable *cordon sanitaire*, had become aware of my presence: they stood in little groups inside the white line painted across the playground, craning their necks to see better. The teachers—all male, I cannot remember a single woman teacher at that school—were equally curious, stealing surreptitious glances at me as they strolled around the playground ostentatiously in pursuit of their arcane supervisory duties. They wore heavy, shabby suits, some with a waistcoat, reeking of tobacco and sweat. They had the gnarled, hollow-cheeked look of our neighbours who spent their weekends sitting on doorsteps slowly pouring beer into thick glasses.

Almost no communication was possible; my knowledge of English in those early days was limited to the few phrases I had picked up during our weeks in America and on the three-week voyage of the *Marine Phoenix*. I was isolated in the middle of a circle of curious faces, an outsider even though I was standing in the middle of that circle. Several well-meaning boys and teachers attempted to engage me in some form of conversation, but it proved futile. I had no comprehension of what they were saying apart from the odd word. Like myself, these words were so surrounded by sounds I could not comprehend that they could provide no basis for communication. It was then, I think, that I began to recognise an aspect of Australian culture which I did not acknowledge fully until many years later, at a time when I began to think a good deal about the differences between cultures and about the impact of an unfamiliar culture on the outsider. It was this: Australians, at least the children and adults of the inner western and southern suburbs of Sydney in the 1940s, employed a very restricted repertoire of gestures—body language, in the jargon of the seventies and eighties. The faces staring at me, even those that attempted to draw me out of that circle of isolation, were impassive, their hands immobile. You could not 'read' their intentions, especially if you were the product of a culture which habitually employed exaggerated gestures, smiles and other facial expressions. Those sinewy children and gnarled middle-aged men were inscrutable in their curiosity, just as I, no doubt, proved incomprehensible to them in my brightly coloured parrot-garb.

At length a boy pulled on the school bell. I was shown where to stand for assembly while we saluted the flag, promised to honour the King and to obey God—though I understood none of that at the time. We marched into a classroom where someone showed me where to sit. My education had begun.

I cannot adequately describe the sense of total desolation that descended on me during those first days. I can state my condition: I understood almost nothing of what went on around me—none of the instructions the teacher seemed to be giving; nor the significance of the map he unrolled in order to explain something; nor the radio broadcast to which we had to listen. These things may be stated; but I find it impossible to convey the experience of living in a state of almost total incomprehension, of being cast into a group governed by elaborate rules and mechanisms which you cannot comprehend. I was surrounded by a world where things happened, where things were done, where certain actions had consequences, without possessing any ability to discover what was expected of me. What was the strange chant that the class took up at one point? Why did one of the boys get called out to the front to receive a couple of whacks with a stick? What was the point of the teacher's joke that sent the whole class into gales of laughter? Of course there was some trickle of understanding: I realised that the chanting had something to do with numbers; I knew that the boy got whacked because he had been making a great deal of noise. The joke, on the other hand, remained totally incomprehensible—like many migrants and aliens, I was beginning already to nurture a healthy crop of paranoia: was I the butt of that joke?

At the end of the day, as for many days to come, I was in a state of exhaustion. The demands of the relentless but futile struggle to find a chink of understanding in the wall of words, instructions and admonitions confronting me all day had an enervating and unsettling effect. Sometimes I could catch the tone of what was happening. I knew when the teacher was angry, when sarcastic and when placatory, but I had not the least inkling of the circumstances that generated these signals. Perhaps some of Beckett's carefully engineered series of non sequiturs afford a vague analogy to the sense of disorientation I endured that day. When Vladimir and Estragon discuss, with the earnestness of rigorously methodical philosophers, propositions that will not yield any conventional sense, the combination of discomfort and irritation the actors generate in the audience suggests, though only faintly, the quality of my absurdist experience. And I, unlike that audience, had to come back each day.

I was treated with sympathy and a degree of kindness, apart from one or two roughnecks who jeered at me and mocked my prissy ways. People were well-meaning but bemused; they did not know what to do with me. They had been called on to deal with a kind of deaf-mute in striped socks. Their solution to the problem I posed was, in the circumstances, understandable, though at the time it produced much distress and anxiety. I remained in that limbo for a couple of weeks, growing increasingly isolated behind a wall of incomprehension. At least the bright socks had been retired and my road to assimilation had begun. My parents had mustered enough precious clothing-coupons to buy the thick woollen shorts and other heavy gear children wore in that humid, stifling autumn.

Finally, a note addressed to my parents was handed to me one day. At home, with the aid of a dictionary, we deciphered its message: I was to be transferred to a 'Special Class', which everyone at the school, teachers and pupils alike, always referred to as the Idiots' Class. It consisted of a group of thirty or so children of widely varying ages and uniformly abysmal intellectual capacities who were sequestered in it until they reached school-leaving age. What became of them afterwards was, clearly, no concern of the authorities.

My classmates were a collection of largely amiable children, most of them far too handicapped and individual in their freakishness to be conscious of my difference. Several had obviously insisted on wearing clothes as idiosyncratic as mine had been during my first days at school. In retrospect I see them as an oasis of individuality in that undifferentiated, conformist world. They were able to evade the iron rules of convention because, in a sense, they were beyond the bounds of social norms, just as I, in my alienness, fell outside such confines.

Their eccentricities and disabilities revealed themselves in spectacular ways. One large girl spent most of the day sitting impassively at her desk without the least trace of a response or reaction to anything that went on around her, except when an attempt was made to teach us arithmetic. That brought her to life with a dazzling and vivacious display of mental-arithmetic skills. She was a virtuoso in reeling off answers to complicated sums in a clear, high-pitched voice wholly devoid of inflection—or so I got to learn in my last weeks in that class, when I had achieved a degree of understanding. One small boy would occasionally suffer convulsions; people rushed to place a solid object between his teeth once he started writhing and wriggling. A great hulk of a boy who sat next to me—his name was Clive—dribbled constantly from his gaping mouth. Another child threw up at least once a week. Others proved incapable of controlling their bladders; a squeal would, from time to time, go up in the classroom: 'Sir, Neil's wet himself again!'

This chaotic world was supervised by a particularly clapped-out old man. He was even more decrepit and moth-eaten than the other teachers at the school, all of whom had obviously stayed on during the war years, getting older and older, more and more passive, incompetent and irresponsible, refusing to move aside for the hastily trained ex-servicemen who were clamouring for the right to be employed. The old teacher's attempts to suppress the frequent bouts of anarchy that periodically shook the classroom were purely ceremonial. The scene was Dickensian in its exaggerated grotesquerie. The teacher—I have long forgotten his name—would threaten the most dire and bloodcurdling of punishments if we didn't cut it out this moment, immediately. No-one paid any attention because many, like myself at first, did not understand much of what he was saying. He would wait with resignation for that mysterious moment when, as if by common consent, the uproar ceased, and the class was again seated quietly at its desks as models of exemplary behaviour. In those brief periods of truce, he would make an attempt to instruct us.

His pedagogic ambitions were, quite understandably, modest. He tried from time to time to teach us to chant the simpler tables, but only the silent girl was able to master their intricacies. He made occasional attempts to teach us how to spell some of the words in the thin, grey-covered primers in use at the time, or to get us to read in chorus a page from *The School Magazine*. None of his attempts met with much success; most of our days were taken up with various manual tasks—endlessly marbling sheets of paper, producing miles of French-knitting and hundreds of pom-poms in brightly coloured wool. We enjoyed that hugely; these were always the happiest and most peaceful of times. Sometimes we made simple wooden figures by gluing clothes pegs together, or coloured in crudely stencilled shapes on sheets of yellowing paper. From time to time he tried to teach us a few songs: 'Ho-ro my nut brown maiden' and 'The Maori's Lament'. Occasionally he would give up, staring vacantly through the grimy windows of the classroom at the powerlines outside, until the rising tide of anarchy made him leap to his feet to threaten us with the most fearful thrashings, which he never carried out.

I should probably feel resentment for my seven or eight months' confinement in that Idiots' Class. I have always found it hard, however, to whip up much anger. When I descended on that unsuspecting and unprepared school, which had never experienced anyone as exotic as I was in their eyes, they did, I suppose, the best they could for me. In contemporary Australia there are structures designed to help migrant children learn English and to adjust to their new environment and to alleviate, if that is possible, the anguish and distress most of them experience. Indeed, there are institutions designed specifically to encourage them to retain their native language and culture. Such things were undreamt of in 1947 when people like my parents and I represented the first trickle of non-English-speaking migrants to have reached the country for many years. What else could that decrepit and probably ill-funded institution have done with me? It was, after all, a small suburban school catering for families of no great educational ambition or sophistication, whose children would all leave school as soon as possible to work in factories or to marry at a pathetically early age to become careworn, prematurely aged grandmothers in their early thirties. I was for them no different from the incompetents who were marooned in that class, colouring-in and French-knitting their lives away, because I lacked, as they did, the skills on which the social and economic system was based.

My physical appearance alone excited the curiosity of the people in that school. Otherwise they remained detached and uninterested; no-one showed any inclination to ask about the world I had left—even if I had been able to tell them about it at all coherently. They could not conceive that I was a refugee from Venice and the Midget Theatre, from nights at the opera, and from the arcane social rituals of prewar Central Europe. Such things were meaningless for them. My membership of the Special Class was merely a formal ack-nowledgement of the general predicament my parents and I faced—handicapped and disadvantaged through our inability to communicate, lacking those skills of language that provide the grounds for a community's existence and self-definition. The Australia of 1947 could not have found tolerable the babel of tongues envisaged by the more idealistic contem-porary advocates of multiculturalism.

The school did not, as things turned out, have to face the one problem that would have emerged had we not moved from Hurlstone Park towards the end of the year. Imperceptibly, a miracle had started to occur. I was beginning to learn English, and therefore to possess some knowledge of the world it conveyed, reflected and interpreted. What would have happened if my parents had not found that flat in Epping, thereby allowing me to enter a more conventional stream of education, I have no way of imagining. No-one, as far as I could tell, ever left the Special Class—you stayed there until you had reached the age at which you could be cast out into the world as a well-trained French-knitter and paper-marbler. I dare say that something would have been done about me, for no doubt someone would have discovered that I had a capacity to learn, as most of my classmates sadly did not. Luckily I did not have to wait for that to occur.

How that miracle began is impossible to distinguish from the broader process of learning—learning to recognise the sights, sounds, even the smells of Sydney as soon as some shape and pattern had begun to emerge from the jumble of impressions bombarding us in the course of our first days. I learnt more English, it seems to me, from people in the streets, from signs painted on shop-awnings, from newspaper-posters than I did from the little instruction I received at school. In consequence, the discovery of language is inseparable in my memory from the discovery of a place and its people, or at least those places and their inhabitants that our very restricted familiarity with Sydney offered. I learnt English in the streets and shops of Hurlstone Park, but even more significantly perhaps, from the vantage point of the Strand Arcade in the city.

In their early months in Sydney my parents endeavoured to take up the threads of their old way of life. They lived off their capital while my father looked around for business opportunities. In order to do that you had to have an office. He rented an empty shop on an upper level of the Strand Arcade, a place that was not, at the time, the kitschy essay in nostalgia it has since become. The 'office' was furnished with a desk, two chairs and a metal clothes-rack. My parents spent a great deal of time in that dusty room waiting for opportunity to knock on the door. When it finally knocked, my father was lured into a disastrous venture that relieved him of the residue of our capital in a remarkably short time, forcing him to seek employment as a weaver on the night shift in a large mill, and my mother to learn industrial sewing. In the meantime, the office provided the vantage point from which I learnt a great deal about Sydney. I spent most of my spare time there, looking, wondering and absorbing.

The Sydney we spied from the Strand Arcade has been eloquently recreated by Peter Carey in *Illywhacker*—he locates the Badgery Pet Emporium, that marvellous image of the noisy life of the city in the late forties, in the neighbourhood of the Pitt Street end of the arcade. We observed the chaotic street-life Carey celebrates in his novel. The pavements were crowded with narrow-eyed men in ill-fitting three-piece suits of heavy pinstripe cloth. Many wore sweat-stained pork-pie hats. Most of them carried cameras; they would snap you and hold out a card bearing the address of the studio where you could inspect your likeness. Most people ignored them; the footpaths were littered with discarded pieces of cardboard. The women were also distinguished by extraordinary headgear, grotesque confections, like ziggurats gone wrong, in straw, felt, braid and tulle. Years later my mother discovered the source of these hats in a subterranean salon where customers assembled their own fantasies from the raw material displayed in large containers scattered over the cavernous basement.

We observed this world with fascination, but because we had almost no means of comprehending it—being unable to read what the newspaper-posters were saying or to understand what the paperboys were shouting—we experienced a strange sense of voyeurism. We saw a busy, crowded street-life without much idea of the reason for this hectic activity. In Budapest, a few months earlier, it had been different: there my parents were a part of that equally frenetic scurrying. They too were trying to survive in the confusion of those postwar months. It took some time for us to realise that those narrow-eyed, hollow-cheeked photographers, with curiously distracted expressions on their faces, were returned servicemen desperately trying to make a living with their cameras and pieces of cardboard at a time of widespread unemployment.

At length, however, perplexity was gradually transformed into familiarity. We began to discern a pattern in this seething throng. We got to recognise the faces of the news-vendors on the corner of King Street. The milk bar in Martin Place where a lady virtuoso attracted admiring crowds as she poured milkshakes in a creamy stream from metal containers held high above her head became one of our favourite haunts. We learnt to say 'Tschocolat milk-shek pliz'. We began to grow familiar with the intricacies of the city: we knew where to get certain trams, which trains went from Wynyard and which from St James; we discovered the secrets of the various ferry routes—the large steamers to Manly, the little boats that scudded to the other side of the Harbour, and those which went to all sorts of mysterious and perplexing places.

Eventually the confusing meaninglessness of this world began to be changed into some form of coherence, something that could be understood and tamed. We began to learn the words essential to daily existence. We knew where to go for bread and what the word for bread was; we were no longer restricted to buying only what we could point at. More complex symbols or linguistic forms gradually yielded their secrets, but always in a haphazard manner. We were great cinema-goers in those years. One of the marvels of the cinema is that you can understand and enjoy a great deal of what it has to offer, even if you comprehend practically none of the dialogue. Even advertising-posters contributed to our education. You had only to glance at one of them pasted to the wall of a cinema to know that it was advertising *Gone with the Wind*—now we knew the word for wind. One curious feature of these posters puzzled us and no amount of guesswork would solve their riddle. What was the purpose of those shapes printed in the corners which contained the letter G or A? We discovered their meaning one day when I was refused admission to the Embassy in Castlereagh Street. 'For General Exhibition' and 'For Adults Only' entered our lexicon.

That is how I learnt English; not by any system of instruction but through the piecing together of an infinite number of small, insignificant details, often becoming familiar with peripheral, at times recondite, phrases and expressions well before the essentials were mastered. Slowly the layers of knowledge, the intersection of language and experience, increased. In harmony with the acquisition of language—indeed in a way quite inseparable from it—came a greater familiarity with the world it conveyed. Once more, this was achieved in a wholly random manner. For instance, we soon discovered the beaches in that torrid summer and autumn of 1947, and indulged in the Central-European worship of sunbathing, not recognising the ferocity of the Australian sun, and thus getting burnt to a frazzle on several painful occasions. For some reason, though, the beach we favoured most was Cronulla, a long and inconvenient train trip from Hurlstone Park. Why had we not discovered Manly or Bondi? I remember that someone took us to Cronulla in a car; after that Cronulla was the place we knew and patronised. Much of what we did in those early months was haphazard or the product of whim, chance or ignorance. During our years in Epping, before the momentous day when my father took delivery of a beige Morris Minor, we used to go to Balmoral, which had become our favourite beach, by a roundabout, inconvenient and unreliable route, not realising that there were much easier ways of getting there, just because that was the way we had discovered during our first summer in Epping.

While I was learning English in this laborious and inefficient manner, gradually outstripping the intellectual demands made on me by the Special Class, I embarked on another voyage of discovery: I became for a time a voracious reader. Although I had received almost no formal schooling before coming to Australia, my mother had taught me to read when I was about seven, and also to write after a fashion—though my handwriting has always been vile and difficult to read. I did not take to books, however, until those depressing months in Hurlstone Park, when I needed an escape from the boredom and the nastiness of life at school. Once again I attempted to find consolation in wildly romantic fantasies, the converse of the drab reality of my surroundings. My reading matter was, to say the least, curious. My parents had brought a few books with them—more were on the high seas with our furniture—which formed a staple of reading and re-reading until they were eventually swapped for other books. They were the usual romantic or sensationalist fiction relished by middle-class readers in Europe as much as in Australia. I read anything and everything. If my parents had any misgivings about the suitability of the books I was reading, wisely they said nothing. Dubious stuff was better, after all, than nothing.

I devoured a weird selection of novels. Several were Ruritanian romances in a genre inspired by *The Prisoner of Zenda*. There were a couple of twenties society-sagas in which aristocractic gentlemen, who were usually called Ödön or Aristide, spent a great deal of time eyeing voluptuous *demi-mondaines* through gold-rimmed monocles. One particularly violent book—the source of several disturbed nights—was called *Via Mala*. It described the grim life of a family in a remote Swiss valley who were kept in the most abject bondage by a tyrannical patriarch, the owner of a sawmill. This nasty and brutal tale surfaced one evening not long ago when I watched a German film adaptation of the novel on satellite television in London. I slept peacefully that night.

The book that made the greatest impression on me, though, was an account of the life of Leonardo da Vinci. This was

101

my favourite book; I must have read it a dozen times—I resolutely refused to consign it to the pile of books for barter—yet curiously I have forgotten both the title and the name of the author. I became enamoured of its lurid and no doubt quite fanciful images of Renaissance Italy; these exerted the same magical influence on me as those nights at the opera in the long-distant past of the previous year. I thrilled to the splendours and brutalities of that heroic world. I always envisaged its proud princes and arrogant popes, its brigands lurking on moonlit nights behind a majestic Palladian portico, and its courtesans waiting to ensnare their latest victims within the frame of a gilt proscenium arch, illuminated by the mystery of a theatrical illusion. Once more I was seduced by the highly-coloured fantasies of a world where people lived with intensity, meeting their fate with courage, bravado and even insouciance—an absolute contrast to the drab world of Hurlstone Park and Canterbury Public School, the pitted playground, the crumpled, often foul-smelling teachers in their soiled, sweat-stained clothes, their fingers brown with nicotine, their nails perpetually black with grime.

The effect of this probably unhealthy influence on my emotional and intellectual development is not for me to judge. I know, however, that it played a major part in the alienation I felt from the world in which I was trapped—it also explains in all probability why, in later years, I came to relish the wonders of the more bloodthirsty of the Jacobean playwrights. What I experienced in those months in Hurlstone Park was probably no different from the experience of many imaginative children, but in my case the gulf between an unsatisfactory reality and a thrilling fantasy-life was, I believe, extreme. I became excessively conscious of the ugliness of my surroundings: the rows of mean cottages in treeless streets, the noisome ditch of the Cook's River, the sagging wires slung between termite-infested poles, the sea of red roof-tiles baking in the harsh sunlight.

I grew equally disgusted with the people around me, not only the crumpled teachers, the sinewy boys or the freaks of the Special Class, but also people like the enormous woman, shaking with fat, a cigarette always poking out of the corner of her mouth, who ran our fly-spattered corner-shop. These perfectly ordinary inhabitants of an everyday world filled me with loathing and a sense of anguish that became, or so I imagined, unbearable. Because my command of English was so rudimentary at the time, and my ability to communicate so imprecise and tentative, my despair and isolation were particularly aggravated because I was trapped within my introspective, indeed solipsistic world. If you cannot reach out to the people among whom you are forced to live, it is fatally easy to fall into the error of coming to believe that the lack is in them, that somehow they belong to an inferior order of being. That disastrous and arrogant mistake was to be repeated time and time again by people of my parents' generation, often with appalling consequences, just as it was evident among the elderly customers of the Balkan Grill in London more than a decade after these times.

Inevitably, I am giving here a very precise impression of a complex process which was accompanied by all kinds of doubt, emotional ambiguities and violent changes of mood. The development of these attitudes was neither simple nor direct, and, needless to say, it went by largely unnoticed at the time. Yet it had one curious consequence, apparently the obverse of the despairing sense of otherness I acquired in the course of those months. I was desperately eager to be accepted by people whose language I was beginning to master and habits to understand, because I could envisage no other life except their life. The only alternative to the joyless and mean-spirited world of the streets of Hurlstone Park was the hypocritical, caste-obsessed migrant society where children were expected to offer to kiss Aunti Klári's hand and to employ the linguistic ceremonies of a stifling culture. I felt that I had nothing in common with that over-elaborate way of life. Only in the highly-coloured romances that I devoured during those months, or in the fascination with opera (which had to lie dormant for many years to come) could I safely acknowledge an essential part of my personality, one closer to 'European' models than I would have cared to admit at the time.

Caught in these cross-currents, I embarked on an endeavour (which was to last until I was well into my twenties) to shed every outward sign that had anything to do with my life before coming to Australia—that is to say, to lead a life of mimicry and parody. It may also be that I was eager to discard memories of what had been lost because, from the perspective of the late forties, I knew them to be irrecoverable. Perhaps I was merely perverse in subjecting myself to such all-encompassing voluntary amnesia. Whatever the truth, once I escaped from the Special Class with a minimal but working knowledge of everyday English—sufficient to camouflage the extent of my ignorance—I could address myself to the task of assimilation among the paspalum fields of Epping.

Epping, where we lived until the year I left school, provided an ideal environment for the task of refashioning myself, for unlearning the experiences and discarding the heritage I had brought with me to Australia. Most importantly perhaps, my parents and I had our own home, inadequate though it was in many ways. Nevertheless we occupied a clearly-defined space which was ours as long as we continued to pay the rent and observed the unwritten conventions concerning the Dunnicliffes and their kind. We were no longer in the awkward situation of people living in rented rooms. Our landlady in Hurlstone Park, though a kindly and well-intentioned soul, had made it absolutely clear that she had first call on the kitchen and the bathroom—you could not sing out to her to hurry up before you burst. We spent much of our time keeping out of her way. In Epping we could shut the glass door of the kitchen that served as an entrance, assured of the privacy we needed to recuperate, to deal with our problems and anxieties, or to have noisy rows. This was a place we could live in. We had known better, but we had also known much worse. As a confirmation of our intention to settle, and probably also as a symbolic commemoration of the previous occasion on which we took occupation of a flat, we daubed the walls with fresh kalsomine before we moved in.

School proved much less of a problem than previously. There was no question now of a Special Class. I knew enough English and was sufficiently familiar with the rituals of school life to survive, though (sensibly enough I suppose) I was put into a class a year below my age group. Moreover, on my first day I did not look such a freak as I had when I arrived in the playground of the school in Canterbury. I had long before acquired the required paraphernalia, including a curious green oil-cloth cape to wear on days of torrential rain.

Both teachers and pupils at my new school were more welcoming; they seemed a little more relaxed than those gnarled and sinewy inhabitants of Hurlstone Park. They were less suspicious, inspecting me with something of the wide-eyed curiosity of country people. They found me very strange, of course, but since they lived on the edge of a city which they rarely visited, but which contained very peculiar people, their surprise was gentler, rather muted. They were less intense, slower moving, much less streetwise than the pupils of Canterbury Public School, many of whom were, in all probability, victims of hardship, unemployment and violence. Epping was a more prosperous place. No-one seemed particularly wealthy (or if people were, they were careful to hide it) but no-one seemed underfed or poorly clothed. In this very ordinary, rather dull world I attempted to invent a personality for myself based on what I understood to be the most desirable characteristics of Australian boyhood.

I must have cut a curious figure. I was shorter and darker than the mostly long-limbed, fair-haired boys of Epping. My speech was still heavily marked by the open vowels, separation of syllables and lack of accentuation that make it so hard for Hungarian-speaking people to acquire the stresses, intonations and elisions of Australian English. Though my vocabulary and command of grammar had improved greatly, I was

still confused about idiom, especially the elaborate rules of
schoolboy slang with its subtle distinctions and gradations.
I was entirely ignorant, for instance, about the mythology
and hierarchy of cicadas. I could never remember whether
a Black Prince was more of a find than a Greengrocer—and
in any event, I loathed flying creatures of any kind. I caused
much hilarity by confusing a full-back with a wicketkeeper.
I got into a hopeless muddle over the taxonomy of marbles.
Yet for all that I tried to swagger and lope like the freckled
heroes of the playground. I did my best to imitate their slurred
diphthong-ridden speech. I invented anecdotes of family life
that were parodies of things I had heard people say in the
playground. Yeah, my Dad made heaps on the SP last Satdy.
Geez it was beaut at Terrigal. Of course my bike has gears,
whaddaya think? I was tolerated with an innate courtesy,
but I fooled no-one. The other boys allowed me to tag along,
largely ignoring me, a clown in the retinue of the great ones
of the earth. Occasionally they would throw a crumb of
recognition at me, but I was, and have remained to an extent
ever since, on the outside, never entirely a citizen of the world
in which I lived.

That surrogate existence was, nevertheless, preferable to
the alternative, remaining within the confines of the exile's
world, where the children of my parents' acquaintances were
expected to preserve the polite rituals of well brought-up
Central European children. I dreaded our mercifully infre-
quent visits to Rose Bay or Bellevue Hill. I hated having to
be polite to our hosts and then to be sent off to play with
the children of the household. In part I envied their expensive
toys, their nice rooms, their talk of trips in the family car
and holidays in the Blue Mountains. I came to feel increasingly
isolated from their way of life. One family we visited on
Saturdays or Sundays insisted that their children receive us
in the uniforms of their expensive private schools. Such
sartorial behaviour in Epping would have raised hoots of
derision. In Rose Bay or Bellevue Hill my drill shorts and
cotton shirt (for I quickly outgrew my New York finery)

caused these children to look down their noses at me. These days I occasionally catch sight of the boy—now a balding man in his fifties—in the streets. We pass each other without a flicker of recognition. I see on these occasions the absurd vision of a child on a stifling summer afternoon neatly rigged out in his Cranbrook uniform—jacket, tie and hat—being told by his parents to play with me nicely until it was time to come in for strudel and kugelhopf.

Caught between confusing and contradictory claims which I could not in any way reconcile, when my search for acceptance became less and less distinguishable from discarding old ways, I found consolation, as always, in the world of illusions. I no longer read those well-thumbed Hungarian romances that sustained me in Hurlstone Park. I had not yet discovered music, which was to be a source of fantasy and consolation in later years. Biggles and his like—which was what the decent Australian boy I ached to become read—failed, on the other hand, to engage my interest. I discovered, however, the wonders of Saturday afternoons at the local picture show. This provided an escape from my humdrum life, a brief period of grace during which I could feel entirely at one with my Australian 'friends', accepted at last, even if only provisionally.

The cinema opposite the railway station in Epping served generous fare for threepence—a feature film, a couple of serials, at least one cartoon and, from time to time, a live magic show. The features were mostly Westerns, with the occasional and delightful surprise, like the Technicolor version of *The Phantom of the Opera* which fuelled my opera-mania with its elaborately staged pastiche of Russian grand opera. The serials were of the Superman, Batman or Nasty Nazis variety. Unfortunately I never managed to see every episode of any one of these serials because at some point in the cycle I would be obliged to accompany my parents (with loud and frequent protests) on those dreaded visits to Rose Bay or Bellevue Hill.

On the golden afternoons when I could go to the pictures,

I would walk to the cinema with one or two of the neighbourhood boys who tolerated me—but never of course with those pariahs, the Dunnicliffes—armed with the price of admission and a penny for sweets. Some phenomenally wealthy people had as much as threepence to spend on extras, but the penny I received was close to the going rate. We always sat in the stalls, well to the front. The upstairs, called the Lounge in the parlance of the day, though it charged the same admission, was the preserve of the despised private-school boys, mostly from Newington or Trinity. Nice girls were not allowed to go to the Epping pictures, which their mothers considered a very rough place. They usually went, under heavy supervision, to the more salubrious establishment in East-wood, or even to the city, with afternoon tea at Cahill's to follow.

On most Saturday afternoons the atmosphere inside the cinema was foetid. Several hundred excited children shouted, screamed and stamped their feet while consuming large quantities of Smith's crisps, Jaffas and licorice straps—the last of which could also serve as efficient weapons. During interval the better-off resupplied themselves from the milk bar next door to the theatre. The people behind the counter could be seen bracing themselves for the onslaught of these small-scale barbarians. By the end of the performance the stink of perspiring bodies, the sour, fatty smell of potato crisps and the sickly-sweet perfume of musk had combined to produce an unforgettably nauseating odour. Often in the summer months, after walking home in the hot afternoon glare, excitedly reliving each moment of the show, I would become violently ill with a bilious headache that confined me to bed for much of Sunday.

Most of the films we saw were grainy black-and-white prints in the last stages of decay. They tore frequently, requiring a pause while the projectionist carried out repairs, which always occasioned a chorus of jeers and missiles from the stalls. But nothing could detract from the thrill and the enchantment of watching brave heroes defeat in single-handed combat an entire cavalry of Red Indians or the bulk of the Luftwaffe. We celebrated each Saturday afternoon the eternal victory of justice and nobility over the forces of darkness. Those flickering black-and-white images may not have had the allure of my glorious nights at the opera, of romantic moonlit scenes on the banks of the Nile or in a scented Japanese garden, but they were the next best thing. I shouted and yelled, jumped up and down, cheered and hissed with people who were temporarily my friends. In that world of illusions I had become accepted as a member of the tribe— even though by Monday morning I would be relegated to the ambiguous position of being neither inside nor outside, dwelling in a no-man's-land between the alien and the accepted. These memories of the Saturday afternoon picture show are, for me, emblems of how far one may learn the language and the customs of other people—and also of the point beyond which you cannot claim to belong to your new world, no matter how expertly you have learnt to mimic its ways.

THE
LIVING
DEAD

Unlike those of us who came to Australia as children, many postwar migrants were too old to learn English with any measure of efficiency. They spent their years in Australia in almost complete isolation, indifferent to their surroundings, and, in many instances, totally ignorant of the society in which they nominally lived. My maternal grand-mother, the companion of my days in Venice and at the Midget Theatre, was typical of these unfortunate people.

She arrived in 1949 after an extraordinarily difficult journey for a poorly-educated woman whose experience of the world had not extended farther than the railway line between Vienna and Budapest. In the company of another lady in her fifties, she travelled by train to Paris where they were taken under the wings of an agency charged with helping the thousands of people restlessly moving around Europe in those chaotic years. These people made sure that the two women reached their small hotel, in one of the streets near the Madeleine as far as we could gather from my grand-mother's rather confused accounts of her time in Paris. They took them to the Eiffel Tower, which my grandmother refused to ascend, and also (or so she insisted in the face of any suggestion that she might have been mistaken) to the Paris Opera, where she was outraged by the sight of all those naked women waving fans. She remarked that her father had been wise when he refused to allow her younger sister to accept a scholarship to the Vienna Opera School. If that was what opera was like, she was glad that there had been no naked showgirls in her family.

From Paris they travelled to Cherbourg for the five-day crossing to New York, third class on the *Queen Elizabeth*. They could not find their way to the dining saloon in the ship's maze of passages and corridors and would have gone without food if their cabin-steward had not taken pity on them, supplying them with sandwiches and plates of cold meat. Members of another aid agency deposited them in their hotel room in New York, collecting them a few days later when it was time to leave for San Francisco. Otherwise they were ignored; they spent all their time in the hotel where, mercifully, the staff in the diner understood German. At least they had food. They did not dare to set foot into the hurly-burly of New York's street-life. They travelled to Sydney from San Francisco on an interminable flight aboard a Pan American Clipper. When they arrived both of them said they had never imagined that the world could have been so large.

My grandmother lived in Sydney until she died in the same week that John F. Kennedy was assassinated. Yet she might never have left that village on the border of Austria and Hungary where her father, in his gold-braided cap, supervised the transport of milk to Budapest and Vienna, and insisted that no daughter of his was to become a painted whore on a stage. Neither her experiences during that extraordinary voyage nor her years in Australia made any marked impression on her, or disturbed in any way her characteristic passivity. She remained as she had been all her life. I remember her as totally impassive when we huddled in air-raid shelters with bombs whining all around us, or when she sat beside me on the waters of a cardboard Venice. If anything, life in Australia aggravated that dominant aspect of her character. She lived with us in Epping, later in other parts of Sydney, wholly indifferent to her environment, her gaze turned inwards, perhaps to the world she had left behind, perhaps to the husband she had lost many years before. Nothing engaged her interest or stirred passion within her. She was one of the living dead.

After a time she came to have a few contacts with the world outside. Occasionally she would go to the pictures with us, and managed, at length, to understand enough English to be able to follow a film in a hazy sort of way. In later years television provided a distraction. She could also decipher bits and pieces of print in newspapers and magazines. But she never learnt to speak English, though she had managed by her last years to twist German into configurations that made some sense to English-speaking people. She never went out alone, never travelled farther than the odd day-trip in the car to the Blue Mountains or the Hawkesbury. Mostly she sat at home with the cat, talking to it at great length. She cooked (abominably); she did the mending, sewed occasionally; but most of her time was spent in front of the television, staring at the test pattern if nothing else was available. Sometimes she would go visiting with my parents, but even then, in the company of people of her own kind, she would merely sit and smile. She had lost interest in other people and in conversation. She had no curiosity, no interests. That smile saw her through the few occasions when she had to make a public appearance. I remember her on the day of my graduation, smiling mutely as we chatted with people on the lawn of the quadrangle.

Nevertheless, her life was happier than that of many elderly women who came to Australia in the years after the war. At least she was part of a family, and in the early years was able to make a contribution to its welfare. Others, though they lived with relatives, were isolated not merely from the world outside, but even within their own homes. For many years I had forgotten about one particularly unfortunate old lady until Elizabeth Jolley's *Milk and Honey* raised her ghost for me. I remembered her when reading about the Heimbachs, Jolley's sinister and tragic creatures, whom she places in a dark and mysterious house, where the windows are tightly

shuttered to keep out the harsh Australian sunlight, so allowing them to preserve their carefully nurtured Viennese fantasy
life of music and dumplings.

This old lady's life was even more terrible and claustro-
phobic, largely because it lacked the macabre melodrama of
Jolley's powerful novel. She was probably well into her sixties
when she arrived in Sydney to join her bachelor sons, both
of whom had emigrated before the war. She lived with them
behind perpetually drawn blinds in a small box of a house
in a featureless northern suburb. In that half light she managed
somehow to recreate the atmosphere, even the smell, of a
bourgeois Central European apartment of prewar days. The
furniture, as I remember it, was the usual humdrum stuff
of the fifties, but she covered every table and the backs and
arms of each chair with the elaborate cloths and doilies she
kept on crocheting until she lost her sight entirely. The living
room and the dining room contained far too much furniture,
much more than was needed for three people. Photographs
of long-dead relatives were placed on every available surface.
The few pieces of silver and crystal she had saved from
destruction were displayed on shelves, sideboards and occas-
ional-tables. There were pouffes and footstools everywhere.
Faded pictures in ornate frames hung from the walls. The
smell of frying paprika and onion and the heady aroma of
poppy seed strudel penetrated every corner of that oppressive
little house.

Her sons, the 'boys', did not know what to do with their
elderly and increasingly cantankerous mother. As far as their
story could be pieced together, they had established for themselves, in the years before her arrival, a comfortably dull way
of life. Rumour insisted that they were homosexuals, incest-
uously so according to some of the more evil tongues that
wagged in the espresso-bars of Double Bay and North Sydney.
Both held office jobs of some sort. They played bridge,
collected stamps, went to concerts, and took holidays (always
sharing a room, according to gossip) in seedy Katoomba
guesthouses. They often quarrelled fiercely, with passionate

intensity. They were, in a way, Patrick White's Waldo and Arthur Brown with thick Hungarian accents.

The arrival of the old lady disturbed the delicate equilibrium of their relationship, which was as much sustained by waspish malice as by brotherly love. She was an intrusion into their carefully nurtured ceremonies of enmity and hate. She claimed too much of their attention. They could never be alone now. She never left the house, refusing to visit the doctor's surgery, or to have her eyes tested when her ancient glasses were clearly no longer protection against accidents. She was always falling over things, bumping into the furniture that cluttered the house. On one occasion she had to remain lying on the floor for hours after one of these falls, until her sons returned from their Saturday morning shopping.

The boys' intricately orchestrated quarrels became uncontrollable three-sided battles. Their mother rose to hysterical heights of vindictiveness as she turned now on one of her sons, now on the other, claiming allegiance from each, accusing both of ingratitude, attempting to come between them in her rage and frustration. One Sunday when my parents arrived for afternoon tea, they stood by the front door of the little fibro box, not knowing whether to ring the bell or to go away, while inside the old lady screamed with the voice of one possessed: 'You want me to die! That's what both of you want! You won't have to wait long! I'm going to kill myself now, right now!' There was a fearful clatter, my shaken parents reported after they had returned to our Epping flat, a noise of breaking glass, of crashing furniture, and above it all, the old lady could be heard cursing her sons, calling down eternal damnation on them, while they, bespectacled office-workers that they were, screeched: 'Mummy, Mummy!' My parents turned round and drove home, overcome by worry and guilt. 'What could we have done,' my father asked, 'broken down the door?'

Their story had a grim ending. The old lady did not kill herself on that or on any other occasion. She lived to a great age. Her sons, who had been totally worn down by her presence, sold the house after her death and parted company, each living in a small rented flat far from the other. They passed out of our lives.

The brothers, like my parents, belonged to that group of migrants who were young enough when they came to Australia to learn English with some measure of success, without, however, losing their awkwardness with Australian-born people, or the quaintness generated by their inability to adjust their open-vowelled, unaccented manner of speaking to the intricacies of Australian-English pronunciation. People like them lived, at best, a half-life; they belonged to no society, they were isolated from the world. They frequently seemed grotesque when their uncertain pronunciation, insecure grammar and very confused command of idiom led them into linguistic traps or dead-ends. Of course, they could manage to communicate up to a point; but subtlety and richness of nuance were completely beyond their capacities. They lived in a linguistic limbo. Even their native language came to be transformed in bizarre ways. Over the years all sorts of words crept into my parents' speech for which they knew no equivalents in Hungarian. They subjected numerous English expressions—shopping centre, southerly change, septic tank, service station—to the phonological and grammatical rules of Hungarian, producing at length a private language, incomprehensible in important respects to Hungarian-speakers in other parts of the world.

The lives of these people demonstrated greater variety than the plight of those unfortunate older people who remained trapped within their homes, never daring or, indeed, showing any inclination to explore the society which had adopted them. They were waiting to die. My parents' generation had to make a living. Some achieved this with spectacular success, eventually becoming considerable economic forces within the community, even moving on, in a few cases, to exercise a measure of political influence. They were, however, exceptional, just as the few people of that generation who managed to learn almost no English, remaining confined within their linguistic prisons, were exceptional. The majority, whatever their individual personalities, whether they achieved financial success or stability, or whether, like my parents, they found their life in Australia a constant struggle to survive economically, developed perplexing and ambivalent relationships with their new environment that frequently left them confused, driving many of them into rituals and ceremonies which were often parodies of the social structures of their former lives.

My parents learnt to communicate with some success. My father's English was much more accurate and careful than my mother's, but only at the cost of a slow deliberateness. He spoke in a carefully measured way, with frequent pauses that were often the cause of some embarrassment. I suspect that he translated for much of the time. By contrast, my mother's English was chaotic, observing no known rules, haphazard, with a wild disregard for case, tense and gender. Yet it was a genuine though idiosyncratic language, capable of achieving a considerable range of tone and nuance. My father never really learnt how to communicate emotions, anger, irony or sarcasm; for that reason his English-speaking acquaintances thought of him as an amiable but somewhat dull-witted man. Few had the chance to recognise his ironic relish of the absurdity of life, which I see living on miraculously in my younger son, or the fatalism which generated, as is so often the case, a sombre gaiety—when you finally acknowledge that there is nothing to be done about the awfulness of life, you realise that you might as well laugh at it.

Neither my father nor my mother ever mastered written English. When my wife and I lived in London for a time, I had to translate for her the warm and loving letters they had written to her, in which only the beginning and the end were in English. During my father's disastrous years in business, I was called upon to act as his secretary, amanuensis and typist. On many evenings, instead of attending to the intricate demands of Latin or Algebra, I would sit at a portable typewriter translating into English the best I could, as my father dictated, often at breakneck speed, elaborate business letters filled with jargon of his trade, and couched in a flowery rhetoric appropriate to Hungarian business-life in the 1930s. Fortunately, both of my parents learnt to read English with considerable competence. When my first book of literary criticism was published, they both waded their way through it with swelling pride, even though they knew nothing about its subject matter.

They achieved greater success in learning English or accommodating to their new life than many of their contemporaries, largely because financial circumstancs obliged them to spend most of their life in Australia in those parts of Sydney where there were no substantial expatriate communities. It was only in their last years, when they lived in a flat in Neutral Bay, that they were anywhere near a concentration of Hungarian people of their own generation. By then it was too late: age, ill-health and years spent in places like Epping, Wahroonga and Pennant Hills made their compatriots seem noisy, intrusive, often vulgar and, by the cruellest of ironies, strange and grotesque. They much preferred the few Australian friends they had made, even though such friendships were severely limited by barriers of language and custom. There was little room for intimacy in such relationships.

Their ambivalent attitude towards other migrants had begun to emerge many years before the time they moved to Neutral Bay. Its seeds were sown during those grim early years in Epping. At a time when several among their acquaintances were beginning to amass those considerable fortunes that were to bring them fame, notoriety and opprobrium, my parents had to contend with a harsh life made even harsher by the environment in which they were obliged to endure those hardships. Both worked very hard, often to the point of exhaustion. After the failure of his first business venture, when he had to seek employment as a weaver, my father worked on the night shift for several years. We would see him briefly in the morning, as he returned home, worn out and ashen-faced, just as I was leaving for school and my mother was setting out for Miss Melville's clothing factory. We would meet again for a short time in the afternoon. Weekends were taken up with housework, but for my father sleep had to take precedence over everything else.

After a while he stopped snatching any more than an hour or two of sleep on weekdays. Having worked for several months at the weaving mill, he purchased from his employers three or four broken-down looms which they were about to sell for scrap. He rented a disused bakery at the other end of Epping and spent the daylight hours tinkering with and repairing that decrepit machinery in an attempt to get it into working condition. Eventually he managed to scrape enough capital together to purchase a small quantity of yarn as well as a machine (resembling a miniature ferris wheel) necessary for the preparation of the warp, and another for winding yarn onto bobbins, and attempted to follow his former calling as a manufacturer of fine quality cloth. He continued on the night shift for some time, getting hardly any sleep, looking more and more haggard and aged. We spent most of our weekends at the factory, as we now called the old bakery, my mother and I wandering aimlessly round its interior, or in the overgrown yard, while he adjusted the looms, turning a screw here, loosening a bolt there, trying to tease some life out of worn-out metal and timber.

At last the looms were ready. My father gave notice at the mill, employed a weaver and started manufacturing. My mother stayed on at Miss Melville's for a while to provide us with money to live on, sewing the identical seam on an endless succession of garments, losing a few precious pence of her wages every time the forewoman found a seam unsatisfactory. My father's business kicked on for a few years, but it was doomed from the start. The age of synthetics was at hand: his looms could only weave unfashionable and unwanted worsted cloth.

After my grandmother's arrival, my mother left Miss Melville's. My parents bought a couple of second-hand industrial sewing machines which they installed in the sleepout of the flat. The two women became dressmakers to the neighbourhood; their real income was generated, however, by piecework—unfinished garments delivered twice-weekly by a clothing manufacturer, a dour compatriot, on which they sewed the hems and put in the zip-fasteners. It was terrible work—poorly paid, unutterably tedious, but they were able to work longer hours at home and so made a little more money. The former grande dame who used to point with a fashionably lacquered fingernail at the details of her 'French' couturier's designs, now worked with blunt nails and chapped fingers on ill-designed clothes destined for country stores, or painfully assembled dresses for her clients from patterns purchased at the local haberdashery.

Household chores, which had always been the preserve of servants, proved a dreadful challenge. In the years before my grandmother joined us, my mother had to learn to cook; when her mother took over those duties the standard of our cuisine declined sharply. Washing had to be done at a tub and a huge copper. My mother, a slight, diminutive woman who barely cleared five feet, had to do battle with an enormous cast-iron mangle of the kind that is nowadays seen fetching huge prices in 'folksy' decorator shops. Shopping had to be carried for miles in pelting rain or in blazing sunlight. And, always, there was the shortage of money to add worry and anxiety to fatigue. Often there was not enough to make ends meet. Quite frequently we would fail to hang our milk-can on the nail by the gate. When every child at school was expected to make a donation for some worthy cause, mine was invariably the lowest, sometimes a miserable halfpence. There was no money for luxuries. The Morris Minor, bought on hire-purchase at what were then deemed to be exorbitant rates of interest, was needed as a delivery vehicle—my father had toyed with the idea of buying a 'ute' but decided that he couldn't sink so low. We had a car before we could afford a radio. The radio came only because a doctor ordered me to spend several months in bed with suspected rheumatic fever—which turned out to be flat feet. My parents knew that I had always wanted a radio, and since that incompetent physician had warned them that I might not survive the illness, they contracted into another hire-purchase agreement to lighten what might have been the last months of my life.

In such hard circumstances, there was little inclination towards social life. Nevertheless, my parents retained some contact with several acquaintances, and with one or two families whom they had known for many years. Keeping in touch with these people was neither easy nor pleasant. Most of their acquaintances' economic means far outstripped theirs. Many had already settled comfortably into substantial houses or spacious apartments. Some had begun to develop by the early fifties the flamboyant way of life that was to draw the attention of the Sunday papers to their more outrageous extravagances.

By contrast, we lived in remote and unfashionable Epping. For some years we did not have a car. Visiting involved, therefore, a lengthy and often uncomfortable journey by public transport. And even when my parents accepted an invitation to visit Point Piper or Bellevue Hill, or even Dover Heights or Rose Bay, my mother was always acutely aware of her unfashionable clothes, pitted fingers, poorly-cut hair— in short all the signs of suburban penury. She resented bitterly the way some of these people humiliated her with the poisonous mixture of subtlety and crassness which is characteristic of many Central Europeans. This was to be a source of anguish for many years, the main cause of the terrible crisis in my parents' married life, when my mother grew strident and vituperative about my father's lack of success, his failure to achieve what every Tom, Dick and Harry (or rather Tibi, Frizi and Miki) had achieved so easily. I do not know if her bitterness was increased by the recognition that she was in a sense the biter bit: some of those people who humiliated her so effectively no doubt remembered their own humiliation at the hands of the haughty provincial upstart with her airs and graces, her villa, her servants, her furs and jewels, and were now handing out as much as they could in return.

These experiences embittered my mother to such an extent that in later years, when a slight improvement in our financial situation and the passing of time had ironed out some of the differences between her way of life and that of her compatriots, she remained resentful and suspicious in her dealings with them. Her preoccupation became to celebrate, instead, the superiority of her Australian friends: their modest, unassuming life, and their readiness, as she claimed, to accept you for what you were, rather than for what you were worth. There was considerable truth in this, of course. But she could not allow herself to acknowledge the sad limitations of the friendships she had formed. People were kind to her, well-meaning, at times enchanted by her vivacity (not realising the depths of anger and despair it masked), but all relationships were necessarily circumscribed by insuperable barriers. My parents never progressed beyond a superficial understanding of Australian society. They had neither the skill nor the energy to attempt to learn its ways at all thoroughly.

Their contacts with Australians were, for most of the time, much hampered by their halting command of English and, often enough, by the narrow insularity of some of the people they got to know. In Epping in the late forties and the fifties, it was almost impossible for people as strange and alien as my parents seemed to the isolated and poorly educated inhabitants of that world to form lasting or satisfying relationships. They were strangers in that land, even though they regarded people of their own kind in smart houses and apartments on the other side of the water with a growing sense of distaste. In this way they too were the living dead, restlessly wandering between two worlds.

At length they were driven, despite their disinclination, to seek the company of other expatriates, with whom they did not have to pretend, at least, that all was well in this land of milk and honey. The range of their friends and acquaintances was naturally limited, yet even within that narrow scope they exercised curious and inexplicable choices. They shunned people of similar disposition and personality, often quarrelling with them over a real or an imagined slight, remaining inflexibly vindictive and unforgiving. My mother, especially, elaborated a terrible mythology of insults and betrayals she had endured. These would constantly torment her; she would demean herself by trying to involve others in her resentments. Yet my parents tolerated and forgave others whose behaviour had violated every canon in their code of social conduct, who had exploited them and mocked them behind their backs. One married couple stands out in my memory as representing the extreme effects of this alarmingly neurotic aspect of my parents' behaviour during our Epping years, the blackest and most depressing period of our life in Australia.

The husband's family had been landowners in the district where my mother was born. According to my mother, the extent of their holding had been quite modest but, as happened so often, in his accounts it had grown to vast proportions. They had been ennobled in his grandfather's time through the old monarchy's attempts to pacify as many as possible of its potentially unruly subjects. He went around Sydney aping, in a way he would not have dared back home, what he considered to be aristocratic ways of behaviour. Totally self-centred, rude, offensive beyond endurance, he treated everyone with an exaggerated *hauteur* which would have been farcical had it not been so disgusting. He never spoke but always shouted. He affected a slurring of the 'r's in what he thought was an aristocratic manner—except when, as frequently happened, he got carried away and entirely forgot about it. His every utterance was laced with scatological obscenities of the most revolting kind.

His wife was a meek, nervous woman, years younger than her appalling husband. She was the daughter of a Jewish banker who had managed to save most of his considerable fortune by transferring his assets to Switzerland in the thirties.

Some years later, he even contrived to have his personal possessions—valuable paintings, silver, a priceless collection of Meissen figurines—consigned in a sealed railway wagon to Switzerland at a time when identical wagons were rolling in the other direction, towards Auschwitz and Treblinka, with their human cargo. She lived in awe of her frightful husband, who took every opportunity to shame and humiliate her.

They visited us on Sundays, arriving at lunchtime, but on most occasions, despite his wife's entreaties, the former *grand seigneur* decided to stay on for an evening meal which my parents, in their often difficult financial circumstances, found hard to provide. The whole day would be punctuated by his noisy demands—a glass of water; more of those pickled cucumbers; some coffee; more wine, but not the muck you've been serving. He treated us as his servants, without the least trace of politeness or consideration. Everyone was at his beck and call; he issued orders in a stream of the most distasteful obscenities. He would fart loudly at table, drawing everyone's attention to his skill. He was a dreadful parody of Hofmanns- thal's Baron Ochs (himself a parody) without Hofmannsthal's wit or Strauss's captivating music to redeem him.

His performance usually reached its climax at meal-times. As his wife fiddled nervously with the food on her plate— she ate very little, and spoke less—he would mount a tirade against her stupidity, her sexual inhibitions, her pride. 'She's so proud of herself you'd think there's a feather sticking out of her arse' was his favourite expression. He would invite us to look at her closely; didn't she have a dumb face? And her appearance—she was a mess. Everything about her drew a scathing comment. She would blush deeply, her head sinking lower and lower towards her plate. These execrations would sometimes give way to reminiscences about the world he had lost: his family's hunting lodge, their faithful retainers, golden misty mornings, sleigh-rides on moonlit winter nights—cheap images culled from equally cheap fiction. But the relief afforded by these interludes was short-lived. After a few minutes he would revert to his former theme, growing increasingly strident, constantly trying to catch sight of himself in the mirror above the fireplace of our windowless living room. He would turn his fury on his wife's parents, those filthy Jews, bloodsuckers, living in the lap of luxury in an hotel suite in Lausanne. A pigsty was too good for people who were so lazy they'd shit on the floor rather than take the trouble of going to the bathroom. He would veer off into complicated analyses of his wife's excretory habits, how she wasn't able to produce anything, not the tiniest skerrick, unless she had a box of expensive Swiss chocolates beside her. Dear God, she would end up by bankrupting him— whereas, of course, they lived on her money in a comfortable house in a pleasant suburb.

Why my parents tolerated all this is beyond my comprehension. They claimed that it was out of pity for the unfortunate wife, but that was clearly an insufficient explanation. I suspect that their decision to keep on seeing this couple, providing them with food and drink, when their restricted circle of acquaintances nevertheless contained much less outrageous, altogether more civilised people, was a result of the deep spiritual disturbance produced by their harsh and in many ways joyless life. These were people you could not envy, despite their comfortable financial circumstances. At least they did not treat my mother, who was mortally ashamed of her poverty-stricken appearance, and of the way in which her fingers were covered with evil sores and scabs, with the woundingly contemptuous civility she encountered on the few occasions that we visited our smart friends in the Eastern Suburbs. ('What a sweet dress! Who made it for you?') My parents could even feel superior to the former landowner and his tormented wife. Perhaps they could see themselves, briefly and provisionally, as more fortunate than these emotionally stunted creatures. But the deepest reason for such an odd choice of friends, for their tolerating the intolerable when other much less serious offences were condemned with unforgiving determination, was, I am convinced, that exile, the half-life or living death they were leading, had somehow thrown their emotional and ethical responses entirely out of balance.

Because the world of Epping seemed to them so alien, because they were adrift in an environment to which they found it very difficult to relate, their attitudes towards their own kind—with whom there were fewer barriers of language or custom—lacked the discrimination, even perhaps finesse, they had exercised in their social relations in the past. The spiritual ills of migration and exile manifested themselves in curious and disturbing ways; the dislocation from familiar patterns of life, the absence of that network of social and family relationships which had sustained them and given substance to their existence, produced eccentricities, curious aberrations of behaviour or judgment which revealed themselves, it seems to me, as much in their odd choice of friends as in their financial miscalculations, or in the fantasies they entertained about the possibilities of life in their new land.

The spectral life led by people like my parents, who were by no means entirely cut off from Australian society yet were never quite at ease in it, received its most powerful commemoration in the awesome and alarming figure of Patrick White's Wandering Jew, the tormented Himmelfarb. Neither my parents nor any of their acquaintances approached the intellectual strength of White's extraordinary creation, nor were they capable of enduring the self-scrunity or self-abnegation with which Himmelfarb lacerates himself. His predicament, illuminated by the intense light of White's vision, nevertheless reflects the experiences of those who may have suffered less intensely, yet suffered all the same—even if their sufferings had at times the characteristics of farce rather than high tragedy.

Riders in the Chariot was published in 1961. The date is, to my mind, crucial. This was the time when the confusing and contradictory pressures on people who had come to Australia in the immediate aftermath of the war combined to reveal to them the particular nature of their predicament. They had, by that time, lived in Australia long enough for its critical and disturbing impact to have become somewhat blunted. They had been away from Europe long enough for the irresistible need to escape brutality and horror to be replaced by a tentative nostalgia for a lost world. By that time many had lost the febrile energy that had sustained them through the war years and had allowed them to survive the trials of living in an alien environment. They no longer needed to struggle to learn the basic tools of communication or physical survival. Some had prospered. Many, like my parents, were at least making a living. They could relax their vigilance and the fierce determination to survive that had seen them through the horrors of war and the immediate confusions of migration. Many were exhausted, physically and also spiritually. Consequently, they turned their gaze inwards, restricting their engagement with life, going through the motions of their daily business, but betraying little vitality and no joy. Many held themselves aloof from the largely uncomprehending world in which they were forced to live, while, at the same time, they grew increasingly alienated from their more successful and confident co-exiles—just as Himmelfarb experiences a powerful disgust and nausea as he crosses the Red Sea of the Harbour on his way to the Rosetrees in Paradise East.

Like Himmelfarb, my parents came at this time to be haunted by the past and by an acute sense of loss. What haunted them was, nevertheless, entirely different from those images of a rich Judaeo-Germanic cultural and theological tradition that enter into a complex counterpoint with the mundane world of Sarsaparilla and Barranugli in the pages of *Riders in the Chariot*. They, like many postwar migrants, had lost a brittle, materialistic, entirely secular way of life; consequently their torment was tinged less by a metaphysical guilt of the sort Himmelfarb suffers, and more by regret, nostalgia, and a growing tendency to romanticise the good old prewar days. They searched for substitutes for that lost world, imagining that they found them in two curious institutions of migrant culture that began to emerge in the late fifties, and reached their golden age during the following decade.

Both of these institutions—espresso-bars and holidays in the mountains—proved difficult to transplant into Australian soil. The espresso-bars were a faint echo of that café-culture which reached its zenith in the first thirty years of the century in the fabled institutions of Vienna, Berlin, Prague and Budapest. Those vaulted, gilded, pillared and coffered palaces could not, of course, be replicated in Sydney—though that bastion of 'native' culture, which migrant society rarely if ever patronised, the Cahill's chain of coffee houses, provided, architecturally at least, antipodean versions of such establishments. The espresso-bars of Sydney were much more functional affairs of plate-glass, laminex and plastic, generously endowed with the favoured kidney-shaped furniture of the late fifties. Nor was there any of the heady intellectual talk, the ferment of ideas—at times radical, at times alarmingly reactionary—that distinguished those hives of Central European political and cultural life. The denizens of the Sydney espresso-bars were bereft of ideas; they were beyond politics. Being generally contemptuous of the world in which they had chosen to live, Australian political life rarely engaged their interests, except on those occasions when they could voice their fears that the country would be taken over by the Communists. Like the rest of the nation, they remained generally ignorant of groups of former Nazis and other European right-wing extremists who were attempting at that time to penetrate the fabric of Australian political life.

The earliest espresso-bars were to be found in the Eastern Suburbs, but one eventually opened in North Sydney, and it was there that my parents found a milieu where they could achieve some sort of a communal life, the likes of which they lacked in their humdrum daily existence. The clientele of these establishments was solidy Austro-Hungarian with a sprinkling of other nationalities. They sat on rickety chairs at flimsy tables, drinking glutinous coffee and consuming large quantities of whipped cream, rich custard trapped between sheets of puff pastry, or strudels oozing with sour cherries. The women had a characteristic look that immediately identified them as members of this society. They wore too much jewellery—a legacy of the days when you had to put all your wealth into gold. One lady, notorious among her compatriots, kept on 'losing' valuable rings and bracelets—in planes, on the street, at the cinema—until the insurance companies declared her to be a decidedly bad risk. Their hair, often fiercely tinted, was fashioned into hard shapes resembling crash helmets. Their clothes were made of expensive but excessively colourful stuff. They looked hard and calculating, and many of them were precisely that.

The women were often the driving forces behind their husbands' financial affairs. They were able to strike harder bargains, were generally ruthless and unflinching in their determination to succeed in their business ventures—usually in the rag trade, though frequently branching out into more sophisticated forms of speculation, especially in real estate: blocks of flats, groups of shops for rental, and occasionally development projects of a more ambitious sort. Their husbands gave, on the whole, a gentler, more flabby impression. They favoured suits made of soft, light-grey material, often worn with white shoes at a time when no public significance was attached to such footwear. They would spend hours sitting on those spindly-legged chairs, tieless, their shirts unbuttoned at the top to reveal tufts of greying fur, their jackets slung casually over their shoulders.

In their own eyes they were men of affairs; they boasted about their many successes, their cleverness in outwitting rivals and competitors; they claimed to be utterly contemptuous of anyone who failed to succeed in a dog-eat-dog world. But their wives—keeping alive the pretence of a woman's proper role in life, talking of clothes and scandals, of their children's startling achievements at school, university or in their professions—knew better. They hid behind the mask of Central

European femininity, yet their determination to succeed yielded to none. They courted success with a steely-eyed dedication; they realised, as I think their husbands did not, that the accumulation of wealth—the more substantial the better—was the only avenue of satisfaction open to them in a world where they would always be isolated by barriers of language, social habits and race.

The urge to succeed, to gain and to preserve wealth—all that they valued in life—prompted many of them to embark on very questionable courses of action. Some attempted to continue several common practices of their former way of life, not realising that the world had changed, that they were now living in a very different social climate. Seated around the laminex-topped tables of their favourite cafés, they indulged in the age-old sport of matchmaking, arranging irresistibly suitable marriages for their sons and daughters, for their nieces and nephews, or indeed for any other young people they happened to know. In my twenties I fell victim to one of these campaigns with embarrassing results.

One day an acquaintance of my parents telephoned, asking me to make up a table for bridge. The invitation surprised me. I did not know these people very well and did not care for them in the least, but they were so insistent that I accepted, probably with bad grace. The evening, which I had been dreading throughout the week, proved interminable. I was trapped in an overfurnished living room, constantly urged to taste all manner of costly delicacies, while several groups of middle-aged Hungarians argued vociferously over the best way of making three-no-trumps. Weeks later, after I had mentioned to my parents (probably for the hundredth time) what a crashingly boring evening it had been, the truth came out. That roomful of bridge players was to contain three special guests: an elderly couple and their daughter, who was (unbeknown to my hosts) the sister of one of my good friends from university days. When my parents had pointed out— after a number of coy hints had been dropped—the folly of this attempt at matchmaking, the unfortunate young woman and her parents were quickly warned off, to be replaced by three obliging bridge players culled from the society of the espresso-bars. For many weeks after that disastrous evening, my hostess kept on reminding my mother what a golden opportunity I (a poorly-paid academic without prospects) had thrown away.

A few of the people who began to congregate in these espresso-bars in the late fifties were to achieve spectacular successes which brought them, at times, notoriety well beyond their restricted circle, thereby doing much harm to the esteem in which Australian society held this group. Some, like my parents, were to reel from crisis to financial crisis, always contriving to keep their heads above water, but never finding the security they longed for. By far the greatest number, however, became people of considerable substance—not the fabulous wealth amassed by their notorious compatriots, whom they criticised vehemently while secretly respecting them, yet much greater wealth than many of them had ever known. They had large incomes and a surplus of means that could be spent on luxuries and indulgences. Collectively and individually they formed a not-insignificant force within the economy, yet they had little ambition to engage with any facet of public life.

They directed their economic power inwards, towards various forms of self-indulgence, often to impress their compatriots and fellow exiles. Many lived in spectacularly stylish houses and apartments. They drove expensive cars. They invested considerable sums in furs and jewellery, even though they knew that in Australia these items were not the negotiable commodities they had been in the financially chaotic world from which they came. They began to travel abroad at a time when it was prohibitively expensive, even by sea. Since they trusted none of their employees, being at times pathologically suspicious of even the most obviously honest of people, they preferred to take trips of short duration, travelling by air in those days before the cut-price world of the 747 cattle-trucks. They spent large amounts of money on fares; at their destinations they stayed in the best hotels. In their earlier life a week's holiday in a modest boarding house in Vienna, Rome or Paris represented the usual limit of their ambitions; now they travelled vast distances to stay at the Crillon, the Dorchester and the Waldorf Astoria.

Despite their affluence and readiness to spend, they seemed to experience little satisfaction or stimulation from their enviable way of life. Though they travelled widely, they showed little interest in the places they visited. In Paris their ambition did not extend beyond shopping, strolling along the Champs Elysées and the obligatory visit to the Lido or the Folies Bergères. Some acquaintances of my parents got in touch with me one day when I was living in London in the early sixties. They said that they would like to take me out somewhere; what was there to do in London? They were not interested in any of the suggestions I made—a play, a concert perhaps, or a musical? We ended up at a Hungarian restaurant in Soho which served vile chicken paprika. They complained that London was filthy, boring, that the people were drab and lacking in style. The shops were not much better than at Double Bay, and certainly not a patch on Düsseldorf. How could anyone live in such a hole? Yet back in Sydney, seated around kidney-shaped tables, they and people like them lamented endlessly about the cultural desert in which they were forced to live. In sharp contrast to the much smaller number of prewar migrants from Central Europe, many of whom made a remarkable contribution to the appreciation of the arts, especially music, in this country, these people made almost no attempt to foster cultural life in their new home—apart perhaps from taking out a subscription to the orchestral concerts (where one of the series was nicknamed 'goulash night' by members of the orchestra), which they would usually endure until interval.

They were too much stunned by their wartime experiences, it seems to me, to engage with life in any positive or satisfying way. They were passive even in their greed and acquisitiveness. Though they hungered after success, they had neither the spiritual nor the cultural equipment to channel that success into life-sustaining directions. They were, many of them, empty shells as they sat around tables in espresso-bars chattering, matchmaking, boasting and strutting in their finery. The world outside looked on them with a mixture of amazement and curiosity—it was in the early sixties that wealthy Hungarian Jews entered into the sarcastic mythology of urban Australia.

Only behind the plate-glass windows of their favourite cafés could they find a modicum of solace and a social structure, artificial though it was, to keep at bay the despair many of them experienced and tried to brave with rich clothes and noisy ways. Their plight was to be pitied, though it was easy to ridicule them, because they were suffering the worst afflictions of dislocation. They could not sufficiently master the language or the customs of their new home to dare to move out of their cosy and comfortable ghettoes. They felt trapped. Their old world had ceased to exist. At that time there were considerable dangers in their undertaking even a brief visit to Budapest, Australian passports clutched tightly to indicate that they were, or so they hoped, beyond the reach of the secret police and other potential instruments of terror. Their new world remained hostile and perplexing.

The living death they were obliged to endure was much exacerbated by the absence of a spiritual or at least a satis-fyingly cultural dimension to their lives. The espresso-bars were as close as they could approach to an involvement in a community or a traditional way of life. In this their predicament was very different from that depicted by White in the figure of Himmelfarb. He, at least, feels the acute torment of the loss of a rich communal and spiritual life. His sense of guilt and betrayal, while imposing on him far greater suffering than that experienced by the frequently plangent denizens of the espresso-bars, at least confers a necessary humility on him. People of my parents' acquaintance were also, in a way, much less fortunate than members of several other migrant groups who had come to Australia in the years after the war. Those people had brought with them strong traditions of social life, religious practice, and even of ethnic or tribal loyalties. They were, it is true, frequently locked even more securely into their ghettoes than the more cosmopolitan society among which my parents moved, and many kept alive ugly regional or ethnic enmities (of a kind entirely alien to the culture of the espresso-bars) which still erupt from time to time in public violence.

The world of the espresso-bars at least confined rivalries to a personal level—these people never rioted at soccer games or stormed embassies and consulates. On an emotional and psychological level, however, they lacked the comfort and support that tightly-knit groups, fully aware of their cultural identity, are capable of providing. In such communities the various social and religious rituals, the continuity of the generations, and the sense that individuals are members of a group create a type of communal life far above the capacities of the Twenty-One at Double Bay or Quittner's in North Sydney.

The people of my parents' circle belonged to a totally secularised society. The families of many of them had discarded their Jewishness generations earlier, and had intermarried with people of vague and ill-defined religious backgrounds. Some even came from families that had formally converted to Catholicism in the late eighteenth century, thereby escaping, theoretically at least, the legal restrictions placed on Jews throughout the Austro-Hungarian Empire in the days before their emancipation. For that reason, for many of them who had thought of Judaism as a religion, the Nazi-inspired legal insistence that Jewishness was a race—something to be inherited, rather than embraced or discarded at will—came as a profoundly disturbing shock. They knew of course that in the past members of their families had been reviled, persecuted and slaughtered. But they had given all that away long, long ago—who could remember a time when garberdine was anything other than a type of cloth? They had to suffer the stigma of being Jewish, and the persecution that followed from it, without the spiritual comfort and sustenance that faith or commitment could provide.

Even those who resumed after the war the customs and ceremonies abandoned in their parents' or grandparents' time did so in a sentimental way as a mark of respect for the sufferings of others. In few of them did it rekindle a sense of community, of belonging to a group, from which they could draw psychic sustenance and spiritual nourishment even in adversity. They lived in a limbo where they enjoyed the freedom to indulge themselves in the worst tendencies or characteristics of their heritage, becoming parodies of a way of life that had, for them, entered the realm of sentimental nostalgia. They evolved a mythology of loss, regret and yearning which, over the years, twisted their lives into bizarre and grotesque forms.

The other great institution of this world developed into precisely such an essay in nostalgia, even though its roots were firmly located in the most commonplace of physiological facts. Most Central Europeans find it difficult, almost impossible, to endure a subtropical maritime climate. For many years I believed that, given sufficient time, I would come to tolerate humidity and high temperatures, the oppressive blanket of damp heat that hangs over Sydney for almost half of the year. I now know otherwise—I know that each February will be more difficult than the last. The discomfort of the climate led people, sensibly enough, to seek relief at high altitudes. The cult of the mountain holiday began, therefore, as a purely practical attempt to find a place that would provide a couple of weeks of escape from the heat and humidity of the coast. People soon discovered that on many summer days the Blue Mountains were as bad as Sydney; consequently they explored the high country near Mt Kosciusko. They began spending several weeks at The Chalet at Charlotte Pass, a blessedly cool place just above the tree line, where they could stay in a modest, old-fashioned, rather run-down establishment operated in a half-hearted, lackadaisical manner by the state tourist authority.

We did not join the annual pilgrimage to Charlotte Pass until after the arrival of the beige Morris Minor. It was possible to get there by train and bus, but to all intents and purposes you needed a car. A certain camaraderie arose, therefore, among the people who made the trip each year: they were game enough to undertake the tiring and hazardous drive. For people who had not in most cases learnt to drive a car until middle life, whose eyesight and reflexes were frequently in decline, the drive to Kosciusko provided a daunting prospect. The road between Canberra and Cooma was an appalling ungraded dirt track, pitted with murderous ditches liable at any moment to cause major damage to suspensions and differentials. There were several unmarked level crossings where you were likely at any moment to have a train carrying material for the Snowy Mountains Scheme bearing down on you. From time to time the road would be blocked by a fallen tree. No sign of life was visible anywhere—the Central European fear of empty spaces had full play on that desolate stretch of road. We sighed with relief when we caught sight of the outskirts of Cooma or Canberra.

The last few miles of the mountain road were narrow and unsealed, with treacherous hairpin bends. At many points two cars could not pass; one of them had to reverse into the natural bays that dotted the mountainside, a nerve-racking experience for people who had not, so to speak, been born with a steering wheel in their hands. The descent into The Chalet was a straight, steep gradient. Our Morris could not manage the ascent fully loaded; when we set out for Sydney at the end of our holidays, my mother and I would have to walk up to the road to make it possible for the little engine to chug its way up the hill.

The first summers at Charlotte Pass were merely a prelude to the golden age of mountaineering in the sixties and seventies. Accommodation was primitive; meals were of the standard boarding house variety: clear soup each evening, with peas floating in it one day, slivers of carrot the next, pieces of potato on the third, followed by cold meat and hot vegetables, the mashed potatoes served with an ice-cream scoop according to the demands of immemorial custom. The lounge, where gentlemen were obliged to wear ties, and slacks for ladies were not tolerated, was a dimly lit affair decorated to look like a combination of a hunting lodge and a baronial hall. But it was all bliss.

The air was cool, cold at night with even the occasional flurry of snow. During the day you could sit for hours in a sunny corner protected from the frequently biting winds, soaking up the sunshine in a way that would have been intolerable on the humid coast. At long last a use could be found for those furs rescued from the collapse of the old world or purchased in the affluence of the new. Admittedly there was nothing to do except to talk, to remember other holidays in other mountains long ago, and to play out the rituals of rivalry and enmity transported from the espresso-bars of Double Bay and North Sydney. In that clear air you could form a firm alliance with your mortal enemy of last week, or savour the drama of the ending of a lifelong friendship through a chance remark or a malicious slight. The few genuine Australians, usually weather-beaten bushwalking types, watched with bemusement these strange ceremonies conducted with flailing arms in an outlandish tongue.

The annual holiday in the mountains soon developed into a ritual with its unique mysteries. As the number of people wishing to escape the heat of the city increased, other resorts— hitherto devoted entirely to winter sports, remaining closed for the rest of the year—began to exploit the opportunities offered by this new type of holiday-maker. At Perisher Valley, and later at Thredbo, lodges of sumptuous appointment and outrageous tariffs vied for their custom. An en suite bathroom became obligatory. The *table d'hôte* grew increasingly elaborate with masses of heavy, carbohydrate-rich food that could not be comfortably consumed on the coast. A nostalgia for a European climate was joined by a nostalgia for its food; the cool breeze and soothing sunshine, imported it would seem from another hemisphere, were complemented by the wonders of the cuisine.

Distinctions and discriminations began to enter the rituals of mountain-lore. The fondue at Marritz was deemed to be incomparable, whereas the Matterhorn's cream-cheese pancakes could not be surpassed. One establishment would be censured for its vulgar and flashy clientele. Another had too many families with noisy children. A third was rumoured to be none too clean. Everyone had his favourite place, the merits of which would be defended passionately. Families would pay ceremonial visits to people staying elsewhere in the valley; afterwards, over fondue or sauerbraten, goulash or schnitzel, the shortcomings and inconveniences of those establishments and the vulgarity of their patrons would be dissected and examined with the elegance of a brilliant anatomist. More and more people flocked to the mountains throughout the sixties, eventually robbing the place of some of its former charm and distinction which the pioneers came to remember with affection. And, as a final outrage, the time arrived when Australians outnumbered 'our people' at these resorts.

For some years, though, until age and infirmity kept more and more of these people marooned in their air-conditioned houses and apartments throughout the long summer, this extraordinary society, brought into being by the displacement of relatively large numbers of people from their familiar environment, continued to live out its fantasies among the stunted snow gums of the high country. Women in furs and men in expensive suede jackets would stroll arm-in-arm in front of the Candlelight or the Alpenhorn, whispering confidences, or stressing a point of view with expressive fingers and hands. In the evenings they would sit in well-upholstered lounges, discussing with earnest dedication the fine social distinctions to be drawn between various hostelries: their clients, the standards of service, situation and cuisine. For a few weeks at least they could live again the life they had lost, before they were obliged to return to the alien and incomprehensible world of the coastal plain, where the only thing to do was to make money. For a while they could continue the snobberies and niceties they remembered from former holidays in mountains or by the lakeside. They were keeping alive a dying world. The high, clear air quickened their responses, gave them a feeling of well-being, put a little colour in their sallow cheeks. Their eyes sparkled: they were alive once more. Years later, thinking about the ceremonies and rituals of this grotesque and sad little society, I came to realise how much it resembled that other dying world, the bright-eyed consumptives of Davos in *The Magic Mountain*, a book that few of those people strolling arm-in-arm in the alpine dusk had ever read.

BRITISH
SUBJECTS

On the 29th of August 1952 my father and I took the train to the city, and made our way to the courthouse in Liverpool Street. We crossed an ill-kept yard littered with cigarette butts and torn newspapers, and climbed a short flight of crumbling steps leading to a gloomy vestibule. There we waited on a dark-stained bench, surrounded by groups of glum people, their backs hunched, many staring vacantly at the floor. Court officials busied themselves with clipboards, summoning now one now another of the people sitting around us. Finally my father was called. He went off with the official, leaving me stranded within the curious gaze of several bench-sitters. After a little time the official returned and conducted me into one of the courtrooms. The Stipendiary Magistrate asked me my name and duly recognised my existence. My father had just sworn allegiance to the Queen, and so became an Australian Citizen and British Subject. I, being a minor, crept in as an addendum. My mother, a mere woman, had to wait some months for the privilege of attending a sitting of the Court of Petty Sessions.

In later years, the granting of citizenship through the courts came to be deemed intolerable. Receiving new members into the bosom of the Commonwealth in the company of people caught exceeding the speed-limit or involved in brawls outside pubs was considered inappropriate to the ideals society wished to foster among its new citizens. By the time it was my grand-mother's turn to be led into the fold, naturalisation ceremonies had developed their individual forms and rituals. We put on our best clothes, and drove to the municipal chambers in Hornsby, where she was made a citizen by Sir Edward Hallstrom, zoo patron and manufacturer of refrigerators, who made a platitudinous speech about koalas.

It was a much more civilised ceremony than our appearance some years earlier at the courthouse. Yet that cruder, essentially down-to-earth way of putting an official seal on the newcomer's request to be granted citizenship was, I think, a fundamentally correct way of going about things, even if it acquired unpleasant associations in the seedy world of the lower courts. The people sitting in that depressing vestibule, waiting to be had up on a variety of petty charges, came closer to representing the real world than those fantasies of communal life enacted in town halls and municipal chambers which never quite escaped the sense of make-believe.

There notabilities made fatuous, at times condescending speeches. In later versions of these rituals, about-to-be-admitted members of the tribe were encouraged to deck themselves out in their national costumes. The ranks of New Australians in fancy dress receiving their certificates of naturalisation looked marvellous on colour television, but the custom served only to emphasise their otherness. This was not the real Australia in which traffic-offenders and pub-brawlers play a minor but undeniably real part. Naturalisation ceremonies became operettas, fantasies of multiculturalism, fundamentally irrelevant to the life of the community. Fantasy was the last thing that many migrants needed; they had indulged in far too many to require official sanction for indulging in more. People of my parents' generation, at least, needed to come to terms with the frequently commonplace and at times depressing reality of the world where they had chosen to live. Turning up at the lower courts registered symbolically a desire for an engagement with reality—that you were now entering into the fabric of Australian society, that you had come under the dispensation of the law of the land, with all its benefits as well as its prohibitions.

Nobody congratulated us as we left the courtroom to be replaced by a Drunk and Disorderly or perhaps a Break and Enter. And we, as we stepped out into the winter sunshine, into the messy life of the wrong end of town, felt relief rather than elation. Our last formal ties with a world of brutality and horror had just been broken—though my mother was obliged to languish for a little longer under the technical burden of being a stateless person. The curious and disturbing ambivalence of postwar migrants towards their new home came into particularly clear focus on that occasion. My father was grateful that he had been granted citizenship; he did not feel that he had done Australia a particular favour in deciding to put our relationship with it on a legal and so to speak permanent footing. Yet my parents knew that naturalisation would not substantially alter their difficult and frustrating attempts to come to terms with the world around them, and that they would always remain alien, whatever their legal status.

A couple of years after my father and I made our appearance at the Liverpool Street court, my mother developed certain alarming symptoms which required thorough investigation in hospital. We set out in the blue Hillman Minx that had replaced the little Morris Minor, tense with the anxiety of people who find it almost impossible to deal with the normal disasters of life. My father, at the best of times a carefully diffident driver, took special pains not to cause any distress to my mother, who was one of those people who believe in some sort of mystic magnetic attraction between cars: if two were near each other, they were bound to collide.

On this occasion she was absolutely right. We felt a bang and a jolt as a large car demolished much of the Hillman's boot. The driver, an irate gentleman, who would nowadays be described as tired and emotional, leapt red-faced from his vehicle, and, taking note of our appearance, began abusing my father in the customary jargon of the time with insults about refs, filthy balts and smelly dagoes. We pointed out to him that legally he was at fault. We mentioned that we were on our way to hospital for tests. He calmed down a little, but did not really get off his high horse, telling us that he was a Member of the House of Representatives, a power in the land, not to be crossed lightly. My father produced his driver's licence, and managed to stammer out that this gentleman seemed to be our federal representative. A few days later, having no doubt ascertained the truth of this from the electoral rolls, the MHR sent a large bouquet of flowers with a note on expensively embossed parliamentary stationery offering to pay for repairs, expressing the hope that my mother's tests would prove negative (which they did), and praising the contribution New Australians were making to this great country.

The benefits of citizenship for people like my parents were clearly defined by that episode. They were legal and social, not at all sentimental or emotional. Just because you had been granted a piece of paper with official signatures on it did nothing to alter your appearance or make you feel any more at home in a world which showed many, though rarely extreme, instances of hostility towards you. It gave you, nevertheless, a modicum of protection. For people coming from a world where officialdom had arbitrary and often limitless powers over citizens, such a benefit was of inestimable value. Even so, doubts and perplexities remained. During the various crises of the early years of the cold war, my parents were often alarmed by the possibility that their citizenship might be revoked if Britain, America and therefore Australia declared war on the countries that now lay behind what had come to be called the Iron Curtain. Menzies's attempt to outlaw the Communist Party was a particularly ominous promise of what might come. My father was much relieved when the referendum was defeated; it seemed to him yet another instance of the fundamental good sense and political responsibility of the people of Australia, despite their frequent crassness, insularity and refusal, on a social level, to tolerate other than established ways.

As for me, citizenship by proxy was merely a confirmation of what I thought I had already become: an Australian. Being an Australian implied, of course, adopting the customs of the country, not merely the formal acknowledgment that I was recognised as a potential citizen who would be entitled to vote in elections and to carry a passport in due course. Naturalisation put the finishing touches to my attempt to refashion myself, to suppress my European self, at a time when the structures of European society—to be endured on our holidays in the mountains, or when I was dragged off to visit my parents' friends, or when intolerable creatures like the former landowner came to visit us—seemed to my adolescent self-righteousness entirely offensive and insupportable. My friends' fathers would never be seen walking arm-in-arm in an alpine twilight. Admittedly, I didn't much care for what I saw them doing on the rare occasions when I visited other boys' homes—immersed in the racing-guide on Saturdays, rolling home on Friday evenings cross-eyed from the six o'clock swill, or else pulling weeds out of the front lawn with robot-like concentration. Yet so powerful were the forces driving me to conform, to seek acceptance by this world, that I allowed myself to experience no distaste whatever for its way of life, reserving my anguish and discontent for my tirades (delivered in Hungarian at the top of my voice) to my unfortunate parents about their frightful friends and acquaintances.

I entered a grey period. My adolescence was boring, unsatisfying and obsessed with the need to become indistinguishable from people I took to be genuinely Australian. I even lacked the excitement of being unusual. Epping had got used to me. People may not have been any more kindly disposed towards us who were, for many years, one of the very few 'New Australian' families in the district, but at least we had been around long enough to be remarkable no longer. The greengrocer stopped asking my mother how many budgies she kept every time she bought capsicums. He would even go as far as saying: 'I've got some nice red ones today, Mrs Riemer.' I made a few friends, boys as lonely and lacking in personality as I was, or those who were briefly attracted to the mildly exotic. Such friendships could not develop firm or lasting bonds. My mother used to remark from time to time how strange it was that I was never asked to birthday parties. People in Epping did not give parties—or if they did, they did not invite me. My social life consisted almost entirely of meandering rides on my bike, often alone, sometimes in the company of one or two boys, always ending at the oval where a group of us would stand around watching the inevitable rutting dogs.

I was plump, pimply and wholly uninteresting. I had no accomplishments. Though I managed to keep my head above water at school, I was not particularly good at any subject except Scripture. Since everyone was obliged to attend Scripture lessons, I decided to play it safe, and joined the Church of England class. I found that I had a strange ability to remember recondite bits of Bible-lore for the tests the minister gave us. I almost always got top marks, and on one occasion in primary school a prize of threepence as well, but these achievements never appeared on the term reports. Otherwise I chugged along, content to ape what I understood to be behaviour acceptable to my contempories. I broadened my accent as far as I could manage. I learnt to spit with gusto, though I could never contrive to whistle through my fingers. I feigned an insatiable interest in cricket and football, read the racing guide without any understanding of its arcana, and, for a brief time, became the owner of one half of a pair of boxing gloves purchased in partnership with a boy called Brian. I spent much time with him in his father's shed, taking turns at punching an ancient mattress propped up in a corner.

Because everyone attended Sunday school, I too went to Sunday school at St Alban's Church of England in Epping.

There I was exposed to the joyless puritanism of Low-Church Anglicans. I was even confirmed as a communicant of the Church of England—that I hadn't been baptised seemed to worry no-one—and succumbed to the obligatory religious mania of adolescence. I grew obsessed with my imperfection and fell into the sin of despair. Those in charge of our spiritual welfare impressed on us the powerlessness of the human spirit to achieve salvation. There was not much emphasis on a loving and forgiving God: rather, we were urged to be on a constant guard against the flesh and the devil—one erotic dream and you were gone. I continued to experience the odd erotic dream and considered myself irrevocably lost. Now a sense of religious inadequacy was added to my other shortcomings and failures. Even in the eyes of the Lord I was destined to be an outsider. I gave religion away when I was about seventeen, having followed for several years a chart which guaranteed that if you adhered to it you would eventually have read all of the Bible. The only thing religion did for me was to cram my head full of odd facts that won me Scripture prizes.

I got almost nothing out of school. It taught me a few skills and gave me a reasonable proficiency in French—the only aspect of my school education to have been the source of lasting satisfaction and stimulation. The books we were expected to study—*King Richard's Land*, *Kim*, *Kidnapped*—failed to stir my imagination to life. In the early years of secondary school I persuaded myself that I detested Shakespeare and hated *The Lay of the Last Minstrel*. It was only in my last year at school that I discovered the world of literature, and even that discovery was made in areas somewhat remote from the books we were obliged to study and the way in which they had been taught to us. Before that, I passionately wanted to be the open-faced philistine most of my classmates seemed to be—though as it turned out several had hidden their lights under bushels, whereas I had never kindled mine. I was abominably bad at sports. I was forbidden to sing in the compulsory choir ('Just open and shut your mouth, but do not make a sound!') because I was incapable of holding a tune. I tried to join the debating team but I was outclassed by boys far more articulate and witty. My parents sent me to dancing classes—just as, in another world, in the year before we left Budapest, they had sent me to a fencing academy where on one occasion I sparred with a scion of the great Eszterházy family—but I proved to have two left feet.

I had learnt to mimic with some efficiency the superficial characteristics of Australian adolescence, but it was no more than mimicry, representing nothing fundamental or intrinsic, merely a thin veneer pasted over emptiness. The anguish and self-loathing I experienced through those years were, I am convinced, the product of that aggressively practical-minded, exclusively male society in which I spent my schooldays, a world that allowed no scope for emotions or for the culti-vation of the sensibility. Being the child of a culture where feelings and affection are expressed far more readily than they were in that pragmatic middle-class boys' high school, I suffered (as I now realise) from the suppression of life-sustaining emotional energies—no matter how bizarre their manifestations might have been among the gesticulating patrons of the espresso-bars. The lack of personality that afflicted me when the drab adolescent replaced the multi-coloured freak of Hurlstone Park revealed the extent of my spiritual impoverishment.

In many ways the greatest influences on my life at that time were closer to the world I had tried savagely to deny, the world of the expatriates with their nostalgic memories of Europe. When I was dragged, resentful and complaining, to visit my parents' friends, or on our mountain holidays ('Why can't we go to Terrigal, for goodness sake, like everyone else?'), I was coming into contact with a world I would eventually have to recover—though not in the stunted and grotesque forms in which it survived amongst us. At the time, though, I could not allow myself to admit that such a despised way of life touched in any way on my real self, or had any relevance for what I was hoping to become.

Nevertheless, the old world and its influences were beginning to creep back into my life in unusual and wholly unsuspected ways. The earliest and most powerful warning that Europe—to use a convenient shorthand for complicated states of mind, memories and longings—would not lie down and fade away, came through that discovery of music which proved to be one of the few consolations of those bleak years. It happened quite fortuitously when I was confined to bed with a suspected bout of rheumatic fever. I spent weeks in bed, listening to the radio for most of the day and well into the night. At first my favourite programmes were serials: *Martin's Corner*, *Portia Faces Life*, *Mrs 'Obbs* and *When A Girl Marries*. I also discovered the crooners and songsters of the day: Bing Crosby, Dinah Shore, the Andrews Sisters, Danny Kaye singing 'I've got a loverly bunch of coconuts', and many others whose names I have forgotten. I listened to radio plays, to Parliament and even the river heights when nothing else was available, and to the Quiz Kids, Jack Davey and Bob Dyer.

Through various bouts of illness in my teens, I lay curled up in bed, the Stromberg-Carlson emitting the faint odour of heating bakelite, listening, lost in the wonder of the serials, the quiz shows, the plays. When I saw Woody Allen's *Radio Days* I was immediately taken back to a familiar and well-loved world. One night, quite by chance, I wound the dial round to the ABC, catching the middle of a concert from the Town Hall. Something entirely inexplicable and magical happened. I have forgotten what piece of music the orchestra was playing, but I can still sense, almost as keenly as I did on that night, the sensuous thrill of hearing the sound of an orchestra in full flight transmitted through the tiny loudspeaker of my decidedly low-fidelity radio. I could not understand why 'classical' music, to which I had remained relatively indifferent until that moment, should have exerted such a powerful influence on me on that particular occasion. Perhaps the sound filling my dark room reminded me of the music I had heard emerging from the orchestra pit all those years

147

ago, which at the time had seemed merely an accompaniment to the more substantial magic of the stage. Yet all the orchestral music I had heard until that evening had left me wholly indifferent. After that night my hunger for music became insatiable. I began exploring the classical repertoire, by means of the radio, with a dedication bordering on obsession. To this day, music provides for me greater consolation than words—words are of the mind, but music speaks to the soul.

The discovery of music was, of course, the rediscovery of European ways of life, a means of recognising that the despised world of the expatriates among whom my parents moved from time to time—to my eyes a grotesque and almost entirely contemptible society—embraced values to which I could relate, values that could fill to some extent the spiritual void in which I lived. Music became, moreover, a way of reconciling the two worlds between which I was already dwelling, even though that recognition, too, lay in the future. At the time, music was apparently no more than an escape, a way of finding an alternative to the humdrum life I was leading— a life entirely devoid of emotional satisfaction, of self-confidence or of any shred of fulfilment, yet a way of life I pretended to find wholly desirable.

After a while the sounds coming out of the tiny loud-speaker-cone were not enough. My parents, always more than prepared to indulge me in even the most difficult circumstances, purchased a record-player and several sets of 78s— *The Nutcracker Suite* was, I remember, the first. Buying a musical instrument and paying for tuition was, however, out of the question. I longed for a piano or a violin but knew that I had to keep silent. At one time I bought some music paper and tried to write a symphony by making marks on the staves without any knowledge whatever of the meaning of those mysterious symbols I saw in the few music scores the school library possessed. In adulthood I took music lessons for a year, painfully picking out some easier pieces on my wife's piano. It was, it goes without saying, much too late—

fingers wouldn't respond, a semiquaver-run proved an insurmountable obstacle. I could hear the music, but all I could produce was halting, thumping confusion. I remain a passive consumer of music, just as I had been in my teens.

The radio and the record-player were supplemented when I was fourteen or fifteen by concerts in the Town Hall. In the fifties, tickets for orchestral concerts in Sydney were as hard to obtain as subscriptions to the opera in Budapest had been in 1946. You could, however, queue up for several hours outside the ticket booth on the Town Hall portico and buy places in the organ gallery or better still on bentwood chairs placed at the top of the steps in the Eastern Gallery. Reluctantly my parents occasionally allowed me to travel into the city on a Saturday evening, decked out in my school uniform, to sit in the organ gallery or on those bentwood chairs and experience the excitement of an orchestra in full cry. When I returned, still wide-eyed with enthusiasm, they would wait for me at the station in Epping, worried and concerned whether I would survive safely the hazards of an unescorted trip to the city—our neighbours' suspicions about that godless place had obviously rubbed off on them.

The Town Hall's elaborately coffered ceiling, its dark-stained podium dominated by huge grey organ pipes, like menacing upended cannons, the niches dotting the walls around the galleries, provided the setting for those evenings when I began to discover aspects of European life which were to play a fundamentally important part in my reconciliation of Australia with the world I had left behind. As with my nights at the opera, the performances I heard at the Town Hall—accompanied by the clatter of trams and the screeching of tyres on those stifling humid nights when the side doors were left open to allow some air into the concert hall—did not make as much of an impression on me as the event itself, the fact of being there, of participating in a glamorous way of life. Many of the concerts were conducted by Eugene Goossens—soon to be knighted and then disgraced—and these were in all probability some of the finest performances Sydney

149

has ever heard. But I was insufficiently educated in the ways
of music to know that. For me, as for Thelma Parker in
The Tree of Man, to hear the music was enough; even if the
violins had emitted the most ear-tormenting whine, or the
horns had burped unmusically, or the tympanist had merely
whacked at his drums with all his strength, to have been there
would have satisfied. The connoisseurship of later life has
robbed music of a good deal of its magic for me.

In the audience, whom I would observe sitting in rows
or chatting under the large chandelier of the main foyer during
the interval, I caught sight of elements of Sydney life from
which my parents and I had been almost wholly excluded.
Well-dressed people conversed discreetly, greeted acquaintances with a smile or a wave of the hand. They displayed, in
short, the outward and visible signs of a civilised way of life
as the consumers of high culture, in a way not very different
from the social pantomime enacted amid the gilt of the
Budapest Opera House. Among these people I would occasionally see some of my parents' acquaintances, those people
whom I looked upon as crassly un-Australian, as representatives of that European nonsense which I, as a good citizen
of Epping, thought entirely beyond the pale. Yet there they
were, in the Town Hall, listening to the music I was listening
to, standing in the foyer as the other members of the audience
were doing. At the time I merely noted what I took to be
an anomaly. It did not occur to me that the distinction
between the two worlds of my experience was much less clear-
cut than I had imagined it to be, or that the two might,
indeed, be to some extent reconciled.

Such a recognition lay in the future, when I would make
tentative and at times evasive attempts to allow 'Europe' back
into my life, at first by means of immersion in its culture,
later—quite recently indeed—by the realisation that the allure
of European culture was, in large measure, indistinguishable
from nostalgia for a vanished way of life. Meanwhile I had
to endure the torments and dissatisfactions of adolescence,
its furies and rebellions which could not break out into major

eruptions of self-assertion because, as I came to understand in later years, I could at that time see no possibility of amelioration in my life. It was no use threatening to leave school, to run away to sea, or whatever other fantasies adolescents entertain, because I could not anticipate anything in the future that would guarantee even a small amount of satisfaction except, perhaps, the impossible—becoming Australian not merely spiritually, but in all other respects as well, most importantly in physical appearance. When I became the first boy in my class who had to shave daily, when my chest and back began to sprout the thick black fuzz that made going to the beach a ceremony of acute embarrassment, my depression and despair reached rock bottom.

I now know that this joyless time was not vastly different from the despair and anguish many adolescents around me were enduring. I also know that those stirrings of longing and desire for other ways of life which, as yet, I did not recognise in the least, were beginning to seethe among many of my contemporaries, several of whom I was to come to know well in later years. At the time I blamed all of my sorrows and troubles on the unalterable fact of my difference, on the difficulty I was experiencing in becoming a true Australian, which in essence meant the particular aspect of Australia that Epping represented in its moral, social and cultural horizons.

I felt bitterly resentful that I was trapped in a European family with its quaint and foreign ways. I made my mother's life misery by refusing to take anything but spaghetti and baked bean sandwiches to school for lunch, not realising that those little bits of pasta in a watery tomato sauce that came out of a tin were, themselves, a version of food that only filthy dagoes ate. In public I became violently xenophobic— I recall with particular shame a couple of disgraceful episodes where I tried to join a small, nasty group of boys at school who tormented the two people of Chinese descent among us. It did not occur to me that my discontent was the product equally, if not more, of the world in which I was living, the world I wanted so desperately to accept me as its own. Yet there, in its very midst, in the myths and fantasies of that important aspect of Australian life in the forties and the fifties that I have chosen to describe by the convenient shorthand of 'Epping', lay one of the means of escape, one of the ways in which I was to find something of an identity for myself. It was to provide an alternative to the pedestrian world around me, and a way back to acknowledging my European self through aspirations which I could share with the people among whom I lived. Its source was nothing other than the *bête noire* of modern political and literary polemics: Australia's status as a colonial culture.

It is difficult for those who cannot remember the Australia of the forties and the early fifties to imagine the isolation and introspection of those times. In a world of rapid and relatively cheap travel, in a world, moreover, where images of war, disaster and outrage are transmitted almost instantaneously around the globe, the tyranny of distance—to use Geoffrey Blainey's evocative phrase—has to a large extent been overcome. Back in the forties and fifties—at least in Epping—it was otherwise. People were cut off from the world by an almost complete lack of curiosity about anything outside their immediate experience. My most lasting memories of our early years are not of hostility but of suspicion—the war years had, of course, exaggerated the inward-looking smugness that produced these attitudes. The people of Epping were convinced of the absolute superiority of their dust-blown, paspalum-infested little community. Even the nearby and more affluent suburbs of Cheltenham and Beecroft were looked upon with considerable suspicion. The evil city was unspeakable, to be visited only when absolutely necessary. Melbourne was another world—of interest only on the first Tuesday of November.

People of my generation are probably the last to have any

clear memories of such a life. The title of David Malouf's *The Great World* reveals for us a poignant irony. We are able to remember a time when the great world was no more than a compact backwater of the kind in which Digger Keen is content to spend his life. But unlike Digger, none of our neighbours in Epping had served overseas, none had experienced the menacing life beyond the confines of their comfortable little world. They could not imagine that anyone would have found this paradise anything other than the answer to their fondest dreams. I pretended to myself that I agreed with them; my parents had to learn to disguise their ache, their longing for the old life, and their regret that they had not discovered the palm-fringed Sydney of their fantasies.

Yet the people of Epping, like many Australians of their kind, entertained fantasies of their own. What little they knew of the world consisted of several layers of a mythology about a dream-England to which they hoped one day to return. They often spoke of going 'home'—when asked how long ago they had come 'out', they would look at you in surprise: they were all second, often third generation Australians. Nevertheless, they spoke about the 'old country', and named the dusty streets of their suburb after English counties and towns. The street directory of the districts around Epping reveals a cartographic litany of green fields, dreaming spires and winding lanes.

Everyone was fiercely loyal to the Empire. Photographs of the King and Queen, sometimes even of the two Princesses, decorated many shops, church porches and the classrooms of the school. On Empire Day a huge bonfire was built on an empty block of land near our place. We stood around the blazing pyre of dry wood and old rubber tyres singing 'God Save the King' and 'Land of Hope and Glory' (never 'Advance Australia Fair') while the neighbourhood dogs yapped in fear and ecstasy as children let off tom thumbs, double bungers, skyrockets and volcanoes. The day the King died, the shops, closed in respect, swathed their windows in black cloth. The loudspeaker outside the electrician's, which drew devoted crowds on the first Tuesday of every November, relayed the BBC World Service's broadcast of the funeral to a group of solemn-faced people huddled together in the dark. For the inhabitants of Epping, despite their Australian patriotism, a nostalgic fantasy of England provided as powerful a source of longing and heartache as my parents' yearning for an increasingly imaginary Europe which haunted their memories and disappointments.

England and things British lay at the heart of the educational fabric of this world. We were taught a great deal of English history at school. The maps we studied were, indeed, coloured red for much of the globe. The books we read, the poems we were made to learn and recite all came from England—or if they did not, as in the case of Longfellow's 'The Village Blacksmith', they were deemed to be English by adoption. The few bits of Australian writing that came our way, chiefly 'Bell-birds', were filled with the imagery of English Romantic poetry—though at the time we knew nothing about that. The only 'patriotic' or characteristically Australian verse I remember from that time is 'My Country'. I do not think that 'The Man from Snowy River' or 'Clancy of the Overflow' ever rated more than a mention. The short stories we read were all English, as were those faded essays by Lamb, Hazlitt and Chesterton that spoke of a world we could scarcely understand, but one about which we could entertain many fantasies.

We were made to think of ourselves as the proud heirs of a noble British tradition. England had brought civilisation and Christianity to Australia just as it had tamed the wild Indian subcontinent, which was falling apart under our very eyes because of its people's foolish desire to throw off what they were told by agitators and rabblerousers was the yoke of Empire. We were urged to persuade our parents to contribute to the scheme of sending food parcels to the people 'at home' to see them through their hour of need, just as they had seen us through ours when the forces of evil and darkness threatened our homes and hearths. We were constantly reminded of our privileges, that we lived under the protection of British law, of the British sense of justice and fair play, that our language was the richest and noblest in the world, and that it had produced the greatest writers the world had ever known.

It would be redundant to comment on the emptiness of these political and cultural ideals. In contemporary Australia decrying the 'cultural cringe' of former days has become an essential ritual within an elaborate political mythology. Of course those attitudes were foolish and fundamentally untenable. No-one stressed the brutality of the infant years of the colony; everyone conveniently forgot that it was America, not England, that came to our aid in our time of peril, just as no-one had ever mentioned that the disaster of Gallipoli occurred because the British High Command considered a ragbag collection of Antipodeans even more expendable than its home-grown cannon-folder. Nevertheless, I am growing increasingly aware as those years recede into the past that such a seemingly mindless worship of a distant and arrogant society conferred benefits on Australian life which we have discarded to our cost. At the very least, it provided palliatives for the discontents suffered by people like me, and, as I was later to learn, for some of my Australian-born contemporaries, for whom escape was the only means of dealing with the unsatisfactory and stultifying life they were forced to endure.

One of the chief benefits for people of my generation—and in this respect it did not matter whether you were Australian-born or a newcomer—of this immersion in England and things English was to put us in touch with emotional and aesthetic possibilities which were sadly lacking in our world. It may be true, as Shirley Hazzard noted in *The Transit of Venus*, that we were exposed to much nature poetry which spoke of things entirely beyond our experience; none of us had ever walked through a field of daffodils. Yet we were made aware, at least, of a way of responding to nature which was not possible in our familiar environment. We were city children; the streets of Epping, or of almost every other suburb of Sydney, offered little more than dusty

roadways and well-tended gardens. The bits and pieces of
bushland we knew were generally no more than scrawny scrub,
much of it practically choked by lantana, ivy and morning
glory. Nothing in our environment suggested that nature could
be a source of wonder or consolation, let alone transcendence.

Our teachers and mentors had failed us, by making no effort
whatever to suggest that out there, beyond the Blue Mountains
most of us knew, and beyond the plains that some of us had
visited, was a natural world, certainly unlike Wordsworth's
fields of daffodils or Keats's seasons of mist and mellow
fruitfulness, which could nevertheless inspire awe and ven-
eration. They could not have told us about it; for them it
was merely desert, the awful emptiness of an empty world.
Yet even if we had come to know that world as anything
but hostile and menacing, where were the poems that preserved
and interpreted this world for us, made it meaningful and
allowed it to enter the stream of our imagination?

Had there been a poetry of the Centre, the 'poetic'
experience of that natural world would not have answered
our emotional requirements in the way that English verse was
able to speak to a surprisingly large number of my contemporaries, and to the generations of Australians before them
who were brought up in the same educational and literary
tradition. Adolescence is a time of longing that requires the
consolations of that mixture of gentleness and melancholy
which English nature poetry is uniquely qualified to provoke
in those fortunate enough to have access to the language in
which it is written. Adolescents are often incurably romantic;
their burgeoning sexuality demands to be channelled into areas
of emotions and sensibility where a sense of beauty—a term
entirely absent from modern aesthetics—provides a counter-
poise to the turmoil and confusion of complex psychological
and physiological changes.

Many of these requirements were fulfilled by the literature
of England, and the traditions it preserved, for which
Australian life provided no counterparts. It gave us experiences
and emotions which were not available either in our physical

or in our home-grown literary environment. We knew very little, it is true, about the intellectual traditions of English poetry. We had never read a line of Donne or Marvell; our entire experience of Milton consisted of the sonnet on his blindness. But the magic of 'The splendour falls on castle walls' exerted a powerful influence on us. We saw snowy summits old in story, as well as the glory of wild cataracts, with a vivid immediacy, as if words were capable of stimulating the retina to provide precise images of what they described. The echoes of these beguiling words rolled from soul to soul in more instances than we were prepared to admit to others or even at times to ourselves. True, the experience was vicarious, perhaps gimcrack, like the ecstasy produced in me years before when I sat enthralled in our box at the opera, but Tennyson's words represented for us an essential experience which we could not approach in any other manner. His poetry, and that of Wordsworth, Keats and Shelley (though not Pope, for instance, whom we usually detested), provided an escape from and a consolation for the ugliness and meanness of the world in which we were forced to live. Neither the physical world we inhabited, nor any of the poetry produced by it, could provide such escape or consolation. The windows of my classroom did not give onto a sylvan glade, but looked out on a busy thoroughfare where lorries laboured up a hill past the garish bunting of second-hand car yards. The literature of England conducted us into the world of the romantic imagination which served one of the essential needs of adolescence. It also catered generously for others: a heroic or noble past in which we could participate, and ethical structures to provide models for fantasies, if not for actual life.

These are contentious issues to raise in the current climate of cultural nationalism. The literature we were required to read at school—and those other books to which we were gradually drawn after many of us started to discard our infatuation with a philistine way of life—provided models of loyalty, altruism, courage and perseverance which, once again, appealed strongly to our adolescent need for imaginative structures that seemed to avoid the compromises we were instinctively making in our daily lives. Literature gave us heroes to worship. It gave us, for instance, Henry V, whom many of us got to know by way of Olivier's stirring film, this leading us, in turn, to reconsider our scorn for Shakespeare. It gave us Sidney Carton; it gave us some of Scott's noble and romantic creatures. It gave us, on a more familiar and domestic level, Jane Austen's characters and the world in which they lived, a cosy rural England, where the values of good breeding, politeness, and consideration for others were mixed with the art of conversation and other civilised accomplishments. We were aware of Austen's irony; we may even have been aware that some of her novels contained disturbingly ambivalent father-figures. But the greatest appeal of her novels to many of my contemporaries during our late adolescence lay in their picturesque representation of a way of life that seemed to many of us more attractive and comforting than our humdrum existence. Some of us, of course, devoured Georgette Heyer as well.

In my own case, an immersion in English culture found its focus in a world of illusions, contained by the proscenium arch of a theatre. In this instance it bore no resemblance to the gilded opera theatre in Budapest; it was an attractive though modest hall in Phillip Street which fell victim to the epidemic of demolitions that swept Sydney throughout the sixties and seventies. A Shakespearian repertory company flourished there for some years led by John Alden, a flamboyantly rhetorical actor in the tradition of the actor–managers of the nineteenth century. In front of often makeshift scenery and in costumes that had probably seen service as curtains and bedcovers, the company performed the great plays—*King Lear*, *The Merchant of Venice*, *As You Like It* and even such a relatively difficult and obscure work as *Measure for Measure*, which drew some disparaging comments in the press for its subject matter.

The acting style was largely operatic, the vowels bore no

trace of the despised diphthong. Alden as King Lear raged against his daughters' ingratitude, writhed in his insanity, howled as he staggered onto the stage with Cordelia's lifeless body. As Shylock he rubbed his hands with diabolic glee at the prospect of getting hold of a pound of Antonio's flesh, yet rose to heights of dignity in the court scene where the essential humanity of the predator was suddenly revealed without any suspicion of a 'Yid' accent. Sitting there on Saturday afternoons I was no longer in Sydney, but found myself transported into that fantasy-England which we had been told was our birthright. Everything in that theatre turned its back on the reality that surrounded us. There was no question of making Shakespeare relevant to the audience's immediate experience. The Forest of Arden was a vista of crudely-painted oaks, not the Australian bush. The powerful allure of the theatre reinforced the fundamental nostalgia for a cloud-cuckoo-land England which I shared with my 'native-born' contemporaries of Epping, living in streets named in honour and commemoration of these fantasies.

Such values seem particularly offensive to many sections of contemporary Australian society. Perhaps they represent aspirations which are best discouraged for the sake of equality and social harmony. Our books and the plays we saw, held up as models by our teachers and by other figures of cultural authority, may often have recommended sexist, paternalistic and elitist ideals and patterns of behaviour. They may have mirrored the values of a dominant culture which implicitly suppressed other ways of looking at social, political and religious issues.

For us Ned Kelly was a bandit; Henry VIII, despite his less than admirable domestic life, a Protestant hero; Irish politics during World War One a shameful instance of ingratitude and treachery. We, in our Anglophile, culturally Protestant state schools, never considered what people like the Dunnicliffe boys, who were swallowed by the world of the Christian Brothers after we left primary school, would have made of all this. We were heirs to a noble tradition.

Through the political ties of the Empire and by way of our mystic Britishness, the world of English literature—Wordsworth's Lake District as much as Goldsmith's deserted village, Scott's medieval fantasies as well as Charles Kingsley's thrilling tale of sea-dogs and Empire-builders—became our world and our heritage, even though we lived at the other end of the earth in a scorched land that provided little solace for the romantic agony of adolescence.

Our educational institutions and the type of literature we were called upon to admire, the way in which English history was presented as a steady progression towards the establishment of British justice and fairness throughout the wide world—in England's present and former colonies as much as in the great sister-nation of the United States of America—may be difficult to defend on social and political grounds in the climate of contemporary Australia. The presence of large numbers of people like myself, who became members of this cultural world even more vicariously than our Australian-born contemporaries, probably helped to bring about the decline of these ideals and aspirations. For people like me, and for many of my contemporaries, however, these structures fulfilled emotional and psychic needs which could not be met in any other way.

Current educational and cultural attitudes towards the intellectual climate of Australia in the decade after the end of the war are probably correct in their political and sociological emphases—though I sometimes wonder whether they represent nothing more than the replacement of one rigid orthodoxy by another. But it is clear to me that contemporary educational structures do not cater for the psychic and emotional needs of adolescents in the way that we were able to indulge in the romantic fantasies generated by our immersion in English literature, or by our being made to feel that we were the inheritors of a rich civilisation that exerted its influence over many lands, and in an unbroken chain from the dawn of history to our visually and physically pedestrian present. It gave us ideals; it suggested that we too had a place in a great design. It is just possible that contemporary adolescents may be capable of discovering these essential elements in a specifically Australian context: in their relationship with the 'real' as opposed to the urban or cultivated Australian landscape; in their dedication to environmental issues; in their feeling of kinship with the original inhabitants of the continent who, shamefully, were regarded as savages by our mentors in the late forties and the fifties. Yet they lack the imaginative structures—chiefly in literature—to give substance to their fantasies, longings and torments.

Australia is not a land for romantics. The Australian writing schoolchildren are exposed to nowadays is eminently capable of making them aware of social, economic and political issues to which adolescents should perhaps be exposed in order that they might avoid the mistakes and injustices of the past. They are sensitive to the pressing social and sexual issues of the kind that our prudish mentors constantly swept under the educational carpet. Children now know that the world is larger than the firmly British-biased model that was presented to us in those discredited days. But nothing in the contemporary educational and cultural climate caters for those powerful longings—romantic, idealistic, seeking for beauty which the individual finds hard to recognise or to define— that our membership of the British world provided for us through books, through a version of history, and through models of behaviour which these structures recommended to us. The few locally-grown instances of such romantic idealism, Patrick White's portrayal of Voss for instance, are too constricted by their authors' doubts and alarms about heroic individualism to serve that essential need.

Australians, other than the original inhabitants of this perplexing land, require, for their emotional and indeed spiritual well-being, contacts with a past and with a tradition which they may regard as their own, of the kind that those Aboriginal people who have not become spiritually annihilated by their contact with urban or even rural Australia have been able to retain. We cannot, however, become naturalised Aborigines. In this respect the terrible gulf that I saw between myself, the short and hirsute 'New Australian' adolescent, and my long-limbed, fair-haired contemporaries was not nearly as deep as I or as they had imagined. In essence we belonged to the same world. The differences of language and custom between us, which were a cause of much anguish as I tried to exist between the laconic world of school and the gesticulating society of the espresso-bars and the mountain holidays, were superficial, accidentals only.

Whether we arrived in this country on the *Marine Phoenix* on a stifling day in February 1947, or whether our ancestors had sailed through the Heads on 26 January 1788, past that headland which in 1947 was to display a row of faintly twinkling streetlights, culturally we were all Europeans. 'White' Australia, that terrible and embarrassing term that is to be spoken only in whispers nowadays, is in essence European Australia, whether your forebears were English, Irish, Scottish or that indefinable mix of nationalities, racial strands and ethnic characteristics my parents and I brought with us from the ruins of the Habsburg world. In terms of real Australian culture and history, there is no difference whatever between people who came here in 1788 or 1947, or for that matter in 1991. But the emotional, cultural and spiritual quandary of people like myself, which I am attempting to capture in these pages before they recede from communal memory, refers very particularly to problems and perplexities produced by the fine and in the long view irrelevant differences between one set of European cultures and social habits and another.

The characteristics of Australian society which became for me at first ideals to emulate, later a source of dissatisfaction and frustration, affected equally many 'native-born' Australians whom I got to know in my years at university, people who proved to be as confused and ambivalent about their cultural allegiances as I, the product of an immigrant culture, felt myself uniquely to be. They had to travel the same road as I was obliged to travel. They had to untangle similar riddles and conundrums. Many had to discover their own identity, and in some cases, as in mine, achieve an understanding of what it is to be Australian, in the old world. There the notions of identity, nationality and culture were to provoke among some of my contemporaries responses as extreme, at times, as the rituals of expatriate society in Australia, when Budapest and Vienna gathered at the Twenty-One or beneath the summit of Mt Kosciusko.

It took me many years to discover the essential affinity between my own apparently very particular confusions and ambivalences and those of people who seemed to me to belong to an entirely different order of existence, to be enjoying an altogether greater sense of harmony with the social structures within which they lived. I now know that the difference between myself, in my own eyes a strikingly grotesque representative of an alien way of life, and the confident people who surrounded me at school and in the streets of Epping or Wahroonga, where we went to live in my last year at school, was only of key and register. I was also to learn, to my surprise and mild dismay, that the despised way of life led by my parents' friends and acquaintances was merely an individual response to circumstances to which 'real' Australians, those who staggered home semi-conscious from the pub on Friday nights and many other nights as well, or those who seemed to concentrate their whole attention on cultivating their gardens, were responding with a deep though unrecognised sense of emptiness and spiritual loss.

We are all strangers in the land. We have all been cut off from forces that are necessary for our psychic or spiritual survival. For my parents' society, as much as for me and for the generations of Europeans who have lived in this country, Australia offers political safety and a measure of financial stability. Our material way of life, even for those who fall into the alarmingly growing ranks of the poor and economically disadvantaged, is infinitely superior in many cases to that which we or our forebears sought to escape, or from which they were, in a literal sense, transported. My parents may have lost a brief but spectacular period of affluence, but they gained freedom from the secret police, and from the swift and terrible changes of political climate which could turn you overnight from citizen to pariah. Many of their acquaintances discovered wealth and economic power beyond the wildest dreams they had entertained in their stuffy apartments in Budapest and Vienna, where their only prospects were, literally and metaphorically, the light well or dark courtyard they saw from their windows.

Similarly, the parents, grandparents and great-grandparents of the people I knew at school or was later to know much more fully and intimately at university, discovered a land— whether they had intended to come here or were brought under duress—where they found, eventually at least, plentiful food and a healthy climate in which to grow and prosper physically. The lanky sun-tanned Australian (especially in those innocent days when we knew little about melanomas) kicking a football or driving through the surf became an image of that body-worship which the denizens of the espresso-bars practised in their different ways when they flashed their diamond rings at each other or waxed lyrical over the latest instances of their business cunning and acumen.

European Australians, too, are frequently the living dead. Like the more spectacular manifestations of this condition among the postwar migrant population, they also lack a sustaining tradition, a network of social, religious and tribal ceremonies which are appropriate for the world in which they live. Their paltry rituals—the worship of the body, the pretence of disdain for the life of the imagination (which many of them practise in secret, behind drawn blinds), their dedication to a practial, down-to-earth, no-nonsense view of life—all produce a spiritual desiccation that manifests itself in social practices as ugly as those of the espresso-bar culture of the fifties and the sixties. The spectacles of public crassness, street-violence, the displays of adolescent sexuality visible in every suburb of every Australian city, and the pursuit of mindless pleasures have a particularly Australian accent. But they are as much the product of disorientation, of the suppression of traditions and obligations which had provided, in a different world, sustenance and solace, as the vulgar rituals of the *nouveaux riches* 'reffos' of Double Bay with their flashy 'un-Australian' ostentation and worship of the external signs of affluence.

Throughout the fifties, which were the last years I spent at school and also encompassed my years as a university student, Australian society witnessed an extraordinary conjunction of social, cultural and psychological forces. These were the years in which people like myself, the children of those postwar migrants who were too old even to consider becoming integrated within the society of their new nationality, and the children of 'native-born' Australians, who were themselves in many cases growing alienated from what they saw as their parents' philistine way of life, were discovering a common ground. The fifties and the sixties were the great decades of integration. People like me had achieved acceptance and had become assimilated without, as was certainly true in my case, noticing that the hoped-for miracle had occurred. These were also the years when, at institutions like universities, new and old Australians mixed freely, discovering common concerns, common perplexities and preoccupations. The sad sights of present-day student-life, where Greek sticks with Greek, Vietnamese with Vietnamese, where Arabs are deeply suspicious of, sometimes hostile to non-Arab people taking courses in Islamic studies, did not exist in those golden years to anything like the extent that they are visible nowadays.

We, by contrast, attempted, even if in a halting and pedestrian fashion, to address ourselves to the question of cultural identity, though none of us, I think, thought of it in such specific terms. What made that possible for us was the fact that newcomers like me had gained by this stage a command of English far in excess of what our parents were capable of achieving. We had the skills of communication, consequently we could reach out across the gulf of appearance, experience and custom that separated us from our Australian-born contemporaries, allowing us to discover that we shared many vital concerns and aspirations. We spoke the same language in much more than a lexical or phonological sense. The education we had received, and indeed the education we were receiving in our traditional, British-inspired universities, made us partake of that mystic Britishness which had been inculcated in us at school. The English-speaking world was our oyster. We had the tool to open it, irrespective of our racial or religious origins—or so we thought. We were united by a common desire to explore that world, to use the magical formula printed on our passports—'Australian Citizen and British Subject'—that would allow us to conquer that world. Many of us ached to escape the restrictions and narrowness of Australia.

The escape route, for most of us, whether we were born in Australia or elsewhere, led to Britain: to London or to Oxford or Cambridge, the great cynosures for people of my generation. For many of us, moreover, the question of what we were, or to put it another way, what it means to be Australian, could only be addressed when we had reached our cultural and intellectual homeland. The way in which individuals dealt with that process revealed curious ironies. For many of us, among them people now well known in circles far beyond intellectual and literary institutions, 'homecoming' meant the impossibility of returning to the land in which they were born. For me, by contrast, it became necessary, through a variety of complex circumstances, to come 'home' to a world where I never felt completely at ease, where I never, in fact, felt entirely at home.

HOMECOMING

I went to England in 1960 armed with a travelling scholarship to write a doctoral thesis in English Literature as well as a crisp new passport declaring me an Australian Citizen and British Subject which contained a request from the Governor-General that all courtesies and considerations due to a loyal subject of Her Majesty should be extended to me. As the boat docked at Southampton on a dull October morning, I thought that I had arrived in all senses of the word. I passed through immigration formalities in what seemed a matter of seconds, in sharp contrast to the fate of all those unfortunates we had picked up in Colombo, Aden and Port Said, who were made to form long queues in a separate part of the arrival hall. I remembered that other arrival, in the stifling shed at Woolloomooloo, where my parents' passports were summarily impounded to indicate that their being allowed to enter Australia was merely provisional and even temporary. In Southampton, the immigration official returned my passport, after a cursory examination, with a few mumbled words of welcome. In those golden days you needed no stamp or entry permit, no limit was placed on the length of your stay in the United Kingdom as long as your passport bore, as mine did, the magic formula.

That arrival was the climax to a long and at times painful process that brought me from the Idiots' Class to the doorstep of the great British academic world. I do not remember what fantasies I entertained as I sat in the boat train to Waterloo, clattering past rows of cabbages and a sign reading BEWARE ADDERS, but I was convinced that a career of singular brilliance lay ahead of me. That confidence was inspired not merely by the academic success I had enjoyed at the University of Sydney as a student of English Literature (after a false start with a couple of disastrous years in the Faculty of Medicine). It was much enhanced by the certainty that I had taken my place in Australian society, and had therefore become the recipient of all those privileges that went with the status of being a British Subject.

My undergraduate days in Sydney, after the two nauseating years of cutting open a succession of stinking stingrays and bloated white rabbits, had been a time of awakening. For the first time in my life I had friends whom I could meet on an equal footing, not with those tentative and frequently suspicious steps towards friendship that marked the few relationships I had formed during my schooldays. I now came into contact with people whose cultural and social horizons were not nearly so restricted as those of the people of Epping had been. The complexity of Australia's social fabric was coming gradually to be revealed to me. I met people from many and varied backgrounds. One friend I made in those days—whose friendship I have kept ever since—was the offspring of a wealthy and cultivated family who wore his advantages with grace and modesty. That was something entirely unknown in espresso-bars. I began to enjoy a social life. With my new friends I discovered the heady world of talk—hour after hour, day after day, in coffee shops, in the quadrangle, on the beach, indeed wherever two, three or four of us had gathered. The load of unhappiness had lifted; I was at last able to enjoy life to the full.

These changes were not unconnected with an improvement in my family's way of life. During these years, and for a year or two afterwards, my parents enjoyed a modestly comfortable though by no means reliable income. Our living conditions had improved greatly. In my last year at school we moved from the flat in Epping to a rented duplex in what estate agents called Wahroonga but the caste-conscious inhabitants of that world knew as the much more plebeian suburb of Waitara. Those niceties of social distinction did not worry us greatly. We now had more space, and a pleasant garden (part of which was entirely ours) a telephone, and best of all a septic system which functioned perfectly as long as you remembered to run the pump for two hours each week. The mangle of Epping was replaced by a washing machine, the ice chest by a refrigerator manufactured by the animal-loving knight who was to confer citizenship on my grandmother a year or two later.

At last we were living in a place where our heavy furniture, which had once belonged to my father's family, could be accommodated without making the rooms resemble a furniture store. My mother, who had formerly detested these pieces, now looked at them with considerable pride, eagerly anticipating their hundredth birthday in the late sixties, when they would rise to the status of genuine antiques. The years when she had to spend hours at a rattling sewing machine were, at least for the present, gone. For a short time my parents knew a small measure of peace and security, even though, as once before, several danger signs were visible—my father's business was already on very shaky ground. The battering their emotional life had received during the previous decades left them unequipped to deal with the next round of financial crises they were shortly to face. In the meantime, though, we were content with our lot. I threw myself wholeheartedly into the delights of university life.

The climate of Australian universities in the fifties and sixties—indeed until the days of the war in Vietnam—must seem, from the perspective of the present, naively irresponsible, complacent, and unjustifiably self-confident. Universities were small institutions, catering for people who knew they were privileged because they had gained entry to these places of learning. Having arrived there, you could get to know, even if only superficially, most people who were interesting, or even those who 'mattered'. These institutions were probably no less representative of the spectrum of Australian society than present-day universities. The Commonwealth Scholarship scheme, which ensured free tuition to anyone gaining a relatively modest pass in the school-leaving examinations, made it possible for many people who would otherwise have found it impossible to raise the fees to study at university. The difference between universities then and now was more a matter of attitude and aspiration, of style and fashion, and it lay in the fundamental notion of what a university should stand for.

We were, I suppose, indefensibly conventional and conformist, in outlook as much as in appearance. Some women students still wore hats to lectures; most men wore ties, many appeared in suits as a matter of course. A few radical spirits signalled their independence by sporting open-necked shirts, or turtleneck sweaters in winter; one remarkable woman gained notoriety by coming to lectures in bare feet. Most of us lived at home. Many country people lived in the various colleges, around which an elaborate social hierarchy had evolved. For many of my contemporaries, though of course not for me, life at university was an extension of wider social networks and family associations. The place was like a club: people were connected by family, social and religious ties. They were, nevertheless, able to form associations beyond these relatively well-marked boundaries far more easily than had been possible during their schooldays. Jill Ker Conway, whose upbringing had been relentlessly Protestant, notes in *The Road from Coorain* that she first came into contact with a cultivated Roman Catholic (a woman who became, many years later, my wife) at university, thereby realising how very limited the view of Catholicism implicit in her family's attitudes and prejudices had been.

By and large though, people still retained the habit of congregating in recognisable groups. One was centred on the solid burgher-values of the upper North Shore—the pearls-

and-twin-set brigade, as the women were sometimes known. There was the 'fast' Eastern Suburbs set, and the country people living in the colleges. And there were the Christians of various persuasions trying to convert anyone they could lay their hands on, while, to counterbalance their influence, Libertarians flaunted their daring non-conformism by refusing to wear ties or shoes.

This little world was no less conformist or seemingly un-adventurous in intellectual matters. Though a number of politicians emerged from the ranks of my contemporaries, few of us had much interest in politics beyond a decision to vote Labor or Liberal once we had turned twenty-one. Nor were we much intent on questioning the structures of society either within or beyond the university. Most of us respected what our lecturers and professors—those incredibly learned people in black gowns—stood for, even if we found many of them unutterably boring and stuffy. We were eager to profit from our education, as long as, of course, it did not involve too much work or distraction from the pleasures of life. We accepted without question the shape and structure of our courses of study. Though we were frequently bored by the books we were required to read, or the topics we were obliged to consider, many of us felt that the lack was in us, not in the system. I, for instance, found (and still find) the novels of George Meredith practically unreadable—almost as unreadable as Henry James's and much less rewarding. It did not occur to me to question the prominent place Meredith occupied in our syllabuses, nor to wonder what academic nest a certain lecturer might have been feathering in his insistence that so much Meredith should appear on our reading-lists. In such matters, as in many others, we were very naive when compared with the streetwise undergraduates of the contemporary world.

We saw ourselves as an élite. Within the walls of an institution some of us still referred to as the Varsity, we imagined that culture and civilisation could be preserved against the forces of ignorance and philistinism. We looked upon the place as a custodian of the finer things of life. There were of course rowdies and vulgarians among us. Engineers were, almost to a man, beyond the pale. Medical students could be trusted to get hopelessly drunk and unruly at rugby games or at the wickedly fashionable rowing-club dance held each year on an island in Middle Harbour. Yet a curious bond of affection tied these elements of university life to most others—even including those social butterflies who methodically failed subject after subject, repeating year after year, without the benefit, it is true, of their Commonwealth Scholarships which they forfeited after chalking up the requisite number of failures. Most of us observed the rituals of the institution with religious dedication. We did not set foot on the lawn of the quadrangle until the day we graduated, and we always invaded the city on Commem Day with pranks we thought were the acme of wit and sophistication. We took part in only one demonstration in those years, to demand traffic lights at the dangerous crossing of Parramatta Road in front of the Union Steps. We were horrified when we found out that a notorious 'Red' had tried to turn the demonstration into a political event.

All that was light-years ago. It would be pointless trying to defend those easygoing, naive and self-indulgent days to the politically sophisticated, at times doctrinaire students and academics of the nineties. That world has vanished, perhaps inevitably, under the pressure of a much more complex society which no longer shares the unanimity of goal and aspiration we thought we espoused. Individually it was, nevertheless, a fulfilling time. We grew, we gained intellectual and social skills, and we were, on the whole, at peace with the world. We knew that after we left university there would be jobs for us in a world our parents had sought to make safe for our sake. Few of us had any concerns or alarms about the future; we flourished in that confidence, and, naturally, we also had a whale of a time. We indulged in fantasies of urbanity and sophistication which were often inspired by our immersion in things English and by the English writers we were reading. Some of us mimicked upper-class English speech and manners; an excessively broad Australian accent was to be shunned if at all possible, and even those of us that had attended a certain type of school did our best to avoid saying 'haitch'. Sometimes we sounded like parodies of a poor imitation of Noël Coward's plays. In our fantasy-life we transformed the campus on Parramatta Road into an image of what we thought Oxford or Cambridge must be like.

Above all, we were a community; we had the sense of sharing a privileged world which conferred membership on us irrespective of our background, nationality or religion. Given the tenor of much of Australian society in the fifties, universities were remarkably free of bigotry or race-hatred. In the freemasonry of those marvellous days, men and women formed easy and genuine relationships. Some of us experimented with sex in a mostly mild and uncomplicated way, though there was always much boasting—often transparently fallacious—about our exploits at parties and dances. The friendships we formed were remarkably free of those prejudices which marred many aspects of Australian life. At our parties the sexes were not segregated in the way popular mythology depicts the social practices of the time. We tolerated and felt affection for each other irrespective of gender, religion or race. We were, in short, contented, perhaps improperly so, yet we were generally cheerful—few of us displayed the misery and surliness of contemporary undergraduate life.

The allure this world had for me needs no explanation. Gone were the tensions, anxieties and uncertainties of the past, the incomprehension that met me in the days before university, a time that came to seem in retrospect a living death. I began to lose the dull anonymity of my adolescence. I also began to acquire or to manufacture a viable personality. Much of it was a mixture of silliness and precocity, but it was great fun. Within my limited financial means I started to experiment with a type of dandyism. I also adopted the affectation of drinking black coffee without sugar, and discovered to my amazement that it tasted better that way. My friends and I explored 'unconventional' food of a kind entirely unknown either in my family or in the traditional cuisine of my friends' world. We discovered that curry was not necessarily a handful of Vencat thrown into a mince stew at the last moment, thereby turning the whole unsavoury mess a bilious green. We encountered artichokes but weren't quite sure how they should be eaten. The first time we saw avocados we wondered whether they ought to be cooked.

We attended many balls and dances, mostly at the Trocadero, always carrying, in brown paper bags, the obligatory half-bottle of Pimms for our partners. At the end we always linked hands and performed what we thought was the cancan. Each August we went skiing, staying in a hut above Guthega Dam. The place had no amenities of any sort; we had to walk on skis for the last two or three miles, carrying clothes and provisions for the week. There were no lifts or tows; you climbed laboriously up a small hill, pointed your skis downhill, and fell in a heap at the bottom. Most of the time, we talked endlessly, drank very moderately, listened to long-playing records of Vivaldi, whose music was all the rage, and of Tom Lehrer, which had been smuggled into the country by a few adventurous spirits who had been to America and had dared to run the risk of bringing back wicked banned material.

Surprisingly, given my dismal record in the Faculty of Medicine, I discovered a measure of academic success, despite skipped lectures, despite hastily flung-together essays, despite the other familiar sins of student life. English turned out to be my strongest subject. When friends expressed well-meaning surprise at this, I shrugged it off with a sense of considerable inner pride. Buried somewhere within my consciousness, however, were the first anarchic suspicions about the reason for this success: here was another manifestation of those arts of mimicry which I had acquired in the playground of Canterbury Public School or in the dusty streets of Epping. I found that I could assume a literary or academic personality more easily than I had been able, in the past, to assume the personality of a sports-lover or an expert philistine. Literary and academic matters probably lay closer to my real interests. Yet I was growing conscious during those years that the whole academic business was little more than a game—you played with this notion and that, you assumed a particular set of criteria in one essay and a completely different set in another. In short, I realised that literary criticism is the art of the plausible, not necessarily the pursuit of truth. Nothing in the thirty years I have spent as a teacher and critic of literature has made me substantially revise that point of view.

Playing games with literary and academic concepts could not have taken place, of course, if I had not discovered a genuine love of reading. I had returned to books in my last years at school, after a long drought during which I read as little as possible, resenting the texts we were required to study at school, much preferring comic books or the occasional copy that came my way of a 'dirty' magazine like *Man*. Just as I had thrown myself into the magic world of opera during our last year in Budapest, and as I used to lose myself in those Hungarian romances that provided my only source of fantasy and consolation during our first year in Sydney, and again, as I had become obsessed with music a few years earlier, I spent every moment I could find reading—anything, everything, indiscriminately but voraciously, to the detriment of my studies, my health (or at least so my parents thought) and possibly my sight, for I had to start wearing glasses at this time.

Books were not easy to come by, but the City of Sydney Public Library in the bowels of the Queen Victoria Building (a crumbling pile that housed, besides the library, the offices of the electricity authority and several seedy shops) provided a rich source of treasures. Obtaining books was not merely a ceremony—writing your name and address on borrower's cards, waiting for your turn for certain sought-after books, making sure that the books were returned by the due date—but a strongly sensuous experience as well. I can still smell the characteristic odour of the books that came from that establishment, entirely different from the smell of books from other institutions I was to come to know—Fisher Library at the university, the Reading Room of the British Museum, and the very Gallic perfume of the books in the Bibliothèque Nationale. I would go to the library at least once a week after school, my Globite schoolcase filled with unread Algebra and Chemistry texts, to stock up on yet more books to read into the small hours of the morning with that avidity and enthusiasm which is ours to enjoy for a few years only.

At university this mania for books was channelled into the formal structures of the study of English Literature and Language. It was in that context that I discovered an ability to mimic, to imitate and to parody the world of scholarship and learning. My essays became rhetorical exercises, explorations of how far you could get away with pursuing a line of inquiry or argument which you weren't sure whether you believed to be true or suspected might be nonsense. I became aware of the distinction between reading literature and studying it in a formal context. I was not at all sure that I enjoyed certain great works—the plays of Shakespeare, *Paradise Lost*, Eliot's poetry—for the reason that their greatness and significance were urged on us. This is no doubt the dilemma faced by many students of literature and by practitioners of the craft of criticism as well. In my case it was exacerbated by the strong sense of make-believe that surrounded many aspects of my life, including my essay-writing endeavours.

I enjoyed hugely parodying now this, now another, type of criticism and scholarship. I would twist and contort the contents of an essay just to introduce a phrase I was intent on including at all costs, or to indulge in word games which I alone could recognise. At the same time I found another outlet for these mimic gifts in the student newspaper and in the annual revue staged under the gloomy rafters of the Union Hall. The newspaper was a very flippant affair, not at all concerned with saving the world. The revues were probably more fun for actors and writers than for their audiences, though they were always well attended and even managed at times to make a modest profit. Between them, they provided me with the most telling, and perhaps the most lasting, influences of my student days.

I have not kept any of the stuff I wrote for the paper or for those revues. It was all, I am sure, entirely jejune and pretentious, but I recall two bits of nonsense which revealed, I think, the nature of my obsessions in those years. One was a crossword puzzle I concocted with a friend in which the answer to every clue was LEVEL. The other was a revue sketch, a Chekhovian fantasia for five characters who delivered melancholy monologues of yearning for spring, for the blossoming of the cherry orchard, and recalled how during a great frost many years before the Czarina ordered her portable organ to be wheeled to the middle of the frozen Neva, where she played Bach preludes and fugues in the gathering dusk. The audience, quite understandably, found this farrago almost entirely incomprehensible; they would have walked out in despair, no doubt, had not one of the directors, nowadays a respected librarian and book-reviewer, come up with the idea of having the five characters deliver their monologues as they were attempting to take turns in occupying the four chairs placed on stage.

The crossword puzzle and, more significantly, the Chekhovian extravaganza revealed, it seems to me in retrospect, the almost entirely unrecognised pressures and longings governing my life in those days—pressures and longings that manifested themselves in my infatuation with parodies, word games and mimicry. I was searching for some sort of cultural identity and tradition of my own, closer to the identity I had inherited from the world I had tried so hard in my teens to disown, rather than one assumed in the way my friends and I used to assume disguises for those fancy dress balls that we attended from time to time. I was drawn to a romantic fantasy-Europe—it did not matter that it was nominally Imperial Russia—in which people could display an emotional intensity I could not permit myself in my brittle, parodic 'real' life. I was in fact, though of course I would have been shocked if anyone had suggested it to me, establishing some tentative, hypothetical and entirely provisional bonds with those people who lamented the old life under the clear skies of Charlotte Pass, Perisher and Thredbo, their voices throbbing with emotion as they recalled the pleasures and experiences of a dead world. As my five characters repeated the formula 'Do you remember? Do you remember? . . .' (and this long before *Last Year at Marienbad*) I was both celebrating and savagely punishing that world. I could approach such experiences only obliquely, just as my genuine and committed devotion to English literature and to the language in which it is written found its fullest outlet in parodies and mimicry, a fascination with word games, palindromes, anagrams, acrostics and other 'mechanical' devices like the crossword puzzle with only one word for its solution.

This, I am convinced, is the common condition of people who are obliged to practise a language which they had to learn, rather than one they acquired within the natural rhythms of learning to speak. For us, in a manner easy to identify but difficult precisely to describe, that language, despite the confidence with which we exploit its forms and possibilities, remains external, or merely cerebral, consistently delighting us with its suppleness, the surprising transformations it is capable of undergoing, but rarely, if ever, becoming fully personal in a way that only experiences acquired from the time of early childhood may become deeply personal. This provisional, I am tempted to say almost flirtatious, relationship with language distinguishes several celebrated writers for whom English was a learnt language—Conrad, Nabokov, but most interestingly perhaps Tom Stoppard, with his wild fantasies that cut across the proprieties of language and culture, a writer who is irreverent enough to turn Hamlet into someone who is constantly talking to himself. Something of this cavalier attitude may also be detected in the work of the Polish-born, Melbourne-based writer Ania Walwicz

who fractures English into patterns entirely lacking in punc-
tuation, following no conventions of grammar or syntax,
producing structures devoid of logical meaning but fraught
with suggestion and insinuation, texts which are closer to
music than to 'normal' writing.

A writer whose work I discovered only recently, which made
me recognise very clearly these potentialities and dangers, and
also the implicit freedom in such uses of language, did not
write in English but in French. I find disturbing and curious
analogies between my life and that of Georges Perec, the
author of the highly-esteemed *Life A User's Manual*, who
died in 1982. Perec and I were born within a few days of
each other. Like me, he was a remnant of the polyglot Habsburg world, though his forbears had lived a thousand
kilometres or so to the east of mine, on the borders of Poland
and Russia. Like my family, Perec's was uprooted by the
threats and alarms of the thirties—though unlike my parents,
his had the good sense to get out in time. They did not,
it is true, go far enough. Perec's parents settled in France;
his father died defending it against the Boche, but that act
of patriotism didn't prevent his mother from being put to
death at Auschwitz.

Perec was born in France. Nominally, therefore, French
was his native language, though he was no doubt obliged
to learn it in a way entirely different from that of 'native-
born' French people. It was probably easier for him to learn
French than it was for me to learn English, but he had to
acquire it as an alien, foreign tongue. His great novel, as well
as his other writings (for instance an extraordinary novel,
La Disparition, written entirely without use of the letter 'e')
are notorious for the outrageous liberties they take with the
French language, that revered institution seemingly enshrined
by the decrees of holy writ. *Life A User's Manual*, his masterpiece, is a dazzling display of the most elaborate word games;
its structure is based on an abstruse mathematical formula;
it is, in essence, a layered series of puns, or conceits within
conceits, which dazzle, disconcert and violate, but they also

celebrate the language with which Perec plays in the manner of a true virtuoso. Everything was grist to his mill. When he spent a few weeks in Australia in 1981 he jotted down the names of several Sydney railway stations—Redfern, Tempe, Rockdale, Sutherland, Jannali—and appropriated them for the names of characters in a novel he was writing at the time. Brilliance and virtuosity there are in plenty in Perec's work, but to the unsympathetic, his high-handed manipulation of language seems altogether lacking in respect. It is an outrage, perhaps, against an instrument that should be treated with courtesy and ceremony.

I was attracted to Perec's work as soon as I began reading the English translation of *Life A User's Manual* in 1988. Only gradually did I come to learn, though, the curious ways in which our lives paralleled each other. I kept on discovering odd bits of information well beyond the time I thought I knew the major facts of Perec's life. I was astonished to learn, for instance, that a small hotel in Paris, in a quiet street near the Botanic Gardens, where I recently stayed for a few days on the recommendation of an accommodation guidebook, was situated next door but one to the house where Perec had lived for several years, the place where the bulk of *Life A User's Manual* was written. I am not much given to thinking about the supernatural; I have never seen ghosts or received visitations. But I am disturbed and fascinated by the way I have been drawn, quite fortuitously at times—or so it seems to me—to a writer whose predicament I am able perhaps to understand a little better, certainly more poignantly, than many other people. I feel a particular kinship with a man I never met, whose life was lived in an entirely different part of the world; a man whose intellectual capacity and literary gifts far outweighed mine, and made him one of the most significant figures of my generation.

People like us find it very difficult to write 'straight'; our attitude to language, no matter how adept we may be, must remain to a large extent provisional and jesting—it is not ours in the most intimate or fundamental sense, even if we have no other language to call fully our own—which is certainly the case with me and was also with Perec. We are attracted to the structures of that learnt language, we are infatuated with its suppleness, its capacity to be twisted into surprising and unexpected configurations, but we are, to a considerable extent, emotionally isolated from it. It does not speak to our heart so much as it appeals to our intellect, to that part of our personality which revels in games, puzzles and brain-twisters. We are tempted to use it in an irreverent way.

In some respects Perec must have encountered greater difficulties than those of us who learnt English in Australia, or perhaps even those who learnt French in places like Quebec, Tahiti or Noumea. He lived in a metropolitan culture—one, moreover, which regards its language as a treasured historical monument, not to be tampered with or altered lightly. English has never, at least in my experience, been held in such respect in Australia. In Britain—and especially in the Britain of the early sixties—it was otherwise: the common attitude to English was more respectful, conservative and much more sensitive to its traditional associations. It was not merely that the British were more careful with grammar, syntax and spelling, though that was something I noticed very soon after I arrived in London in 1960. Rather, I began to find that many words and expressions—often to do with the world of nature—carried nuances and distinctions which had been largely discarded in Australia. In the English I learnt in Hurlstone Park and Epping there was precious little difference between paddock and field, creek and stream. I noticed, after I returned to Australia some years later, that a long, straight street in the western suburbs of Sydney is called Railway Crescent. Such oddities made me realise that for Australians English is also an alien language, even though most of them have spoken it all their lives. It is, for them, fundamentally foreign because it encodes experiences and natural phenomena to which they have no access in their daily lives. Someone like me, who had to learn English as a matter of conscious choice, is therefore not entirely isolated from the linguistic experience of 'native' Australians, thereby providing something of a contrast to the predicament of a person like Perec, who was obliged to make his way in a culture which knows that it is the custodian of its language.

Australians are also mimics and parodists; they too—except for those words and expressions which have emerged directly from the experience of living in this land—are given to twisting and altering the language of a distant and increasingly alien culture. Australian English is, in a way, just as much a mixed language as the Hungarian my parents spoke in the last years of their lives, when they had allowed all sorts of English words and expressions to creep into that language to denote experiences for which it had no equivalents. The mimicry Australians practise is, however, largely unconscious. In the course of my golden years as a student at university, when I was beginning to experiment with the capacities of language—though mostly in the secondary or parasitic field of literary study, not in any serious attempt at writing fiction or verse—I, the outsider, was already conscious of the mimicry or tendency towards parody, which is both liberating and highly perilous, that several of my contemporaries were to discover and to exploit once they arrived in England, the end of their particular rainbows.

As the boat train rattled its way from Southampton to Waterloo through the endless suburbs of South London, I did not imagine that England, the land of heart's desire, the country that had become a mystic birthright for people of my generation through our sentimental education into things English, would be the place where the question of my identity would be most severely tested, where I would have to ask myself who I was and what I hoped to become. I thought I had come 'home', in the way that the people of Epping had dreamt of going 'home'. I imagined that the facility I had acquired in my years in Australia, my ability to mimic the speech, customs and rituals of the land, would make me welcome in the Mother Country as a worthy representative of *my* nation. I felt more Australian as the train pulled in at the station than I had ever felt in my life—especially since I knew that there was little danger here of being stopped by someone in the street who would say to me: 'Andris, how *arr* you? How's sings goink wiz your dear mozer and fazer?'

My self-confidence reached a climax as I took my place in the taxi queue outside the station. Here I was, with my suitcases and cabin-trunk, waiting for a London taxi among genuine English people—though as I listened to the conversations around me I became aware that many fellow-queuers spoke with suspiciously Australian and South African intonations. At length my turn came; I gave the driver the address of the bedsit a friend had found for me near Marble Arch— he didn't call me 'Guv', but I let that pass—and off we went. The London that unrolled in front of my eyes through the murk of an October afternoon had the familiarity of an old friend you hadn't seen for a long time. Now we were on Waterloo Bridge. There was Big Ben, and over there the dome of St Paul's. Here was Buckingham Palace, with The Mall stretching away towards what must be Trafalgar Square; surely if I craned my neck I could catch sight of Nelson on top of his column. The London of the books we had read, of the games of Monopoly we had played, of the verses about Christopher Robin and Alice my friends had remembered from their childhood, was revealed in its full three-dimensional substance through the window of a London cab. I had come home.

That confidence and elation were to take something of a battering in the weeks that followed. I discovered that living in a bedsit had its curious and nagging miseries. It was difficult to sleep, work, cook and wash in the one room. The gas meter was constantly hungry for shilling pieces in the course of an increasingly cold autumn, at a time when the Royal Mint had somehow managed to underestimate once more the demand for those coins. I missed home—without quite realising what that implied. Yet I was, and remained for the next two and a half years, on the crest of a wave; the joys of living in London far outweighed its irritations and inconveniences.

I spent far too much of my scholarship money on theatres and concerts, and had to be bailed out by my parents with bank drafts. The British Museum Reading Room, especially that holy of holies, the North Library (recently commemorated by A. S. Byatt in *Possession*), widened my circle of acquaintances beyond the expatriate community in which anyone like me—without family connections in England or introductions to the sort of people that might ask you to stay for the weekend—was forced to move. It provided, moreover, a passing parade of notabilities: celebrated scholars to whom you were sometimes introduced; an angry-faced Russian count who claimed to have been connected with Ottoline Morrell; and one day I saw a frail figure in an overlarge topcoat and homburg hat shepherded into the North Library by respectful officials to inspect a large folio waiting for him on a stand at the back of the room. That mournful figure turned out to be T. S. Eliot. There were many other delights. Walking at weekends on Hampstead Heath was a joy in almost any kind of weather. In summer I used to go for day-trips with my friends affluent enough to own motor cars to Winchester and Salisbury, to Bath and Tintern Abbey. All in all, life was good; my progress towards fulfilment that had begun as soon as I had left the Faculty of Medicine in Sydney (or to put it more accurately after it had decided it wanted no more of me) continued on its apparently predetermined path.

Yet all was not well. I fancied for a while that my life of mimicry would reap considerable rewards. There was no need in London to attempt to refashion myself in the way that I had tried so desperately and unsuccessfully in Epping in earlier years. I had become, I convinced myself, an educated and reasonably cultivated Australian. Part consciously, part subconsciously, I attempted nevertheless to adjust my behaviour—as did most of my Australian friends and acquaintances—to what we imagined would be more acceptable to a British way of life. There were, in those years, considerable numbers of Australians living more or less permanently in Earl's Court (known to all as Kangaroo Valley) who seemed intent on giving exaggerated displays of those national characteristics which were soon to be immortalised in Bazza McKenzie. We wanted nothing of that. On the contrary, we tried to model ourselves on those people we knew or knew about in Sydney who seemed to us particularly 'British', even under the fierce Australian sun: people like Sir Stephen Roberts, the vice chancellor of the university, who always wore striped trousers with a black jacket and spoke in well-rounded vowels. We, too, tried to adjust our accents, not realising that we fooled no-one, or that our vocabulary gave us away almost instantly, no matter how posh our accents might have sounded to our own ears. I also bought a three-piece suit from a bespoke tailor as well as the first umbrella I had ever owned.

Some of my friends could, after a few months of living in London, give a passable imitation of Englishness, which they managed to sustain for an hour or two before the truth became apparent—'Oh, you're from Orstralia, are you?' I had no such luck. The first words the supervisor of my doctoral thesis spoke to me, after looking at my curriculum vitae, were to ask whether I thought I would be able to manage English. We became close friends in later years, especially after he took up an appointment in an Australian university. But he never lost, I think, his sense of mild surprise that my university should have considered me a proper incumbent of a travelling scholarship to undertake research in English literature, of all things. That was the first warning of difficulties to come, just as it was my first inkling of the essential insularity of English people when it comes to the question of non-English-speakers' ability to learn the nuances and subtleties of their language. Perhaps they are right to think this; I am in no position to judge. In Australia, nevertheless, I had been able to get away with it more easily than English people were willing to allow me on their home ground.

It was foolish to imagine, of course, that I could pass myself off as an Australian in that society. I learnt very quickly that it was not prudent to say to people 'I am Australian' or 'I come from Australia'. They would invariably look at me with surprise and bewilderment. 'But you don't look Australian,' they would say, quite accurately. 'And you don't sound like one,' many would add. I soon became cautious, and adopted the formula 'I live in Australia' as a way of overcoming these difficulties. That, in turn, caused even more problems. People would begin to wonder what I was: Indian? Egyptian? South African?—everything, anything, but never Hungarian, or even Austrian, Czech, Polish or Romanian. The closest anyone ever got to my origins was the woman who was convinced, no matter what I said, that I came from Italy; and from the tone of her voice it was obvious that she had somewhere well south of Rome in mind.

And yet I never felt more acutely, even at times embarrassingly, Australian than in those years in London. The way I walked, the way I wore my clothes (despite the three-piece suit and the furled umbrella), the way my skin had taken colour from the strong Australian sun, all brought Australia to mind, no matter how hard I tried to mimic the life I saw around me in the streets, in the Underground, or in the foyer of the Royal Opera House, where I went whenever I could afford to, and sometimes even when I could not. More curiously still, I began to experience a certain nostalgia for a place that had always seemed to me alien and hostile, despite my feverish attempts in adolescence to become a part of it.

My first Christmas in England, despite the illuminations in Regent Street, despite the brief flurry of snow that fell decorously on Christmas Eve, made me yearn for the long days and intense heat of those Australian Christmases when my parents and I used to swelter in our Epping flat or enjoyed the bright sunshine and cool breezes of Mt Kosciusko.

Whenever I caught sight of an Australian scene in a film or on television, I would experience something of the sensation my parents used to feel on the rare occasions (apart from a couple of notorious weeks in 1956) when photographs of Budapest appeared in a newspaper or magazine. The day the afternoon papers featured a large picture of the Harbour Bridge, to accompany a story about a severe earth-tremor that, according to them, caused widespread panic in Sydney, I felt a curious satisfaction that my little corner of the world had at last gained the recognition it deserved.

Even more curiously, I began to read and to develop an interest in Australian writing during those London years. Back in Sydney I had confined my reading, curricular and extra-curricular, to English and European writers, with a very small sprinkling of Americans. I was, after all, a British Subject for whom only the best would do—and the best in matters literary did not include a few bushwhackers, which was more or less my notion of Australian writers. At school, it is true, I had read *The Fortunes of Richard Mahony*, which made a tremendous impression on me—I wrote a gushing essay on it, only to be reproved for not tempering my enthusiasm with judgment. Since I knew that Henry Handel Richardson had spent the greater part of her life in Germany and England, the trilogy seemed to me the exception that proved the rule I had invented about the inferiority of 'home-grown' literature.

I came to Australian writing quite fortuitously by way of *Riders in the Chariot*. I saw a copy modestly displayed in Foyle's window in 1961. On impulse I bought it and found myself, as did so many others, both enthralled and profoundly disturbed by White's vision. Here was something I had not experienced before: a book that spoke about a world I knew, and even more significantly a book which articulated my doubts and misgivings about that world. I knew Barranugli and Sarsaparilla—those dusty semi-rural suburbs around Baulkham Hills and Castle Hill which we passed every time we drove to the Blue Mountains by what was known in Epping as the back road. I fancied that the model for Xanadu must have been that crumbling baronial estate (later to become the new site for the King's School) on Pennant Hills Road which we passed every time we went to Parramatta. Beyond the piquancy of these moments of recognition—when literature no longer dealt with the distant and the unknown, but with the immediate and the familiar—lay the thrill of finding an assessment of life in Australia which was very far removed from the smug self-satisfaction of the citizens of Epping (and also in a way of the more sophisticated denizens of Wahroonga) and much closer to the anguish and dismay that my parents and I had experienced. As the novel laid bare the hypocrisy and pretentiousness of the Mrs Flacks and Mrs Jolleys of that society, as it tore to shreds their suburban proprieties and snobberies, I felt that White was speaking to me, in the soft English light, about a world where I had experienced much of the distaste he seemed to be expressing towards such a life and towards such people.

Within the rich texture of the novel I found something else that surprised and delighted me as much as its bleak vision of the awfulness of Australian suburbia. I was not ready yet to consider sympathetically the plight of the dispossessed as it is reflected in the terrible figure of Himmelfarb. But I was more than ready to respond to White's venomous portrait of people I thought I knew only too well: the Rosetrees of Paradise East. The dreadful irony of this escaped me entirely at the time. I recognised the gesticulating world of the espresso-bars in Harry and Shirl; but I did not realise that White was also describing people like myself, people who thought that they could refashion themselves, in the same way that Harry and Shirl had tried to transform themselves from Rosenbaum to Rosetree.

Riders in the Chariot kindled an interest in White. Instead of attending to *A Study of the Life and Works of James Shirley*, the verbose doctoral thesis I was writing, I read as much White as was available in England in those years before the Nobel Prize. His appeal was intimately connected with the fact that he seemed to me to be looking at Australian life from the perspective of a European. The ubiquitous sense of alienation—which I later learnt was perhaps more immediately the product of White's personal difficulties in what he saw as a bigoted and unrelenting world—appealed to my sense of alienation from Australia, despite the fact that I was beginning to experience in my London life a certain nostalgia for things Australian. White, like Richardson before him, seemed, once more, an exception. I did not recognise, or was not willing to concede, that despite his jaundiced and despairing view of Australian life, he represented something fundamental to the Australian psyche, not merely the point of view of someone as alien as myself.

For many years I read few other Australian writers, at least until 1967 when I published an essay on *The Tree of Man* in which I played language games with the text of that novel, trying to cram as many analogies with European 'high culture' (Jung, Shakespeare, the medieval mystics, Wagner) as that 'bucolic' Australian book would bear. To my surprise I found that the novel could bear quite a lot, and that people took note of what I had to say, even if they disagreed with it wildly—as White did, in his characteristic way. After that I began to develop a genuine interest in a number of other contemporary novelists and poets. To this day, however, the literature of urban Australia speaks to me much more eloquently than what is, arguably, the literature of the 'real' Australia. Despite my admiration for the skill and wit of Les A. Murray, I have to admit that his verse celebrates a world that I do not understand or like very much. *Such Is Life* interests me as a curious development of the chivalric and pastoral romances of the sixteenth century—it has, after all, both horses and sheep in it—yet as a document of human life, the reason why so many people whose judgment I respect are drawn to it, Furphy's book remains, unfortunately, closed to me.

At the same time as I was discovering a tentative and provisional Australianness within myself, quite different from
my deliberate programme of assimilation of earlier years, I
began to experience a pull in the other direction—towards
Europe, towards that part of my heritage which I had
attempted strenuously to suppress. Like all but the most
English-obsessed of the young Australians living in London
at the time, I discovered the joys of Continental Europe, at
least as far as it was possible within my limited financial
means. That was the beginning of a tentative, evasive and
entirely devious journey that was to take me back, thirty years
later, to the place where I was born, to the perspective—
much as I am reluctant to admit, even now—from which
a part of me will always look at the world.

In the early sixties I went to Paris several times with groups
of friends. Getting there was a curious adventure in itself.
We took a bus from the station at Victoria to one of the
wartime airfields near the Channel; then flew in a shuddering
and probably entirely unsafe DC-3 to Beauvais; finally another
bus dumped us in the Place de la République. We usually
stayed in a small and not entirely clean hotel near the
Panthéon, where a notice in the dark entrance passage (you
could not call it a lobby) respectfully requested patrons to
give forty-eight hours' notice if a bath were required. I looked
for that hotel on a recent visit to Paris: it is still there, but
its entrance is now surrounded by a facing of marble, and
you can just catch sight of a rubber plant through the glass
door plastered with recommendations from various tourist
organisations and the emblems of credit cards.

We explored the many delights of Paris from that seedy
little hotel where Madame poked her head angrily through
a contraption (not unlike the servery-hatches in the dining
rooms of our parents' houses) whenever we rang the night-
bell after the official and much publicised locking-up time.
We sat in the gods of the Opéra and inspected the wigs of
the singers and the floorboards of the stage. Dutifully, we
shuffled past the Mona Lisa. We watched while a film was

being made on the banks of the Seine opposite Notre Dame. Afterwards we climbed one of the towers of the cathedral to marvel at the panorama below us. Like my grandmother years before, I refused to go up the Eiffel Tower—vertigo runs in my family. One evening we ignored the whistles warning us that the gates of the Tuileries Gardens were about to be locked, and were obliged to clamber over the stone balustrade above the Place de la Concorde, under the suspicious gaze of the gendarmerie, much to the amusement of a busload of Algerian tourists. One golden afternoon, as we sat, happy and exhausted, outside a down-at-heels café, we noticed the banner headlines announcing the death of Marilyn Monroe.

Two or three times in the course of those years I took longer trips with a friend, nowadays a respected federal politician who, in those days, proved an invaluable guide to the glories and quirks of things English, as well as a patient and sympathetic audience for my many alarms, uncertainties and confusions. He was also the fortunate custodian of a company car. We meandered through France and Italy, criss-crossed Germany and Switzerland, and saw the midnight sun in Norway. But my most significant visits to the Continent were those I took alone: to Italy, sitting up all night in a train, as my father had done decades before, arriving exhausted and red-eyed; to France and to Germany. But I never went anywhere near the geographic (if not spiritual) world that had bred me. Going to Hungary in those years of the Berlin Wall and the Cuban Missile Crisis was out of the question. It strikes me as curious and significant, though, that I always avoided Vienna, the city which was home for my mother's family much more than Budapest—nominally the capital of the nation whose citizens they became after the Great War— had ever been. I thought I had found, instead, a spiritual home in Western Europe. On those solitary visits I could somehow merge into a world that was comfortingly familiar and entirely exhilarating, even though I was seeing these places for the first time in my life.

I responded instinctively to European cities. Their vistas, the way of life their inhabitants led (even if, as in Italy, my understanding of their language was very limited) were strangely familiar and sympathetic to me. I came to think that this life, centred on the great public spaces from which dwellings, shops, offices and theatres fanned out in broad avenues or snaked in crooked lanes, was somehow my true heritage. I had no memories of a peaceful or affluent city of the kind that I found in Paris, Milan, Amsterdam, Munich and Stockholm or even in a delightfully messy and chaotic Rome. My memories of European city-life were entirely those of cities under threat, as Budapest had been before the worst of the bombing, or else cities which had been gutted by the obscenity of war, as we found during the few days we spent in a ruined Vienna in 1946. And yet these sparkling cities, with their traffic jams, their cafés, the glimpses of domestic life you could catch behind the windows of a first-floor flat at dusk, before the owners had thought of drawing the curtains, the Sunday ritual of walking in parks and municipal gardens in one's best clothes, were familiar, comforting and desirable. My responses during my first hours in cities I had never previously visited were the direct opposite of my parents' alarmed disorientation as we drove through Sydney on that February day in 1947.

Europe, especially Italy, also gave me living, substantial images of that world of romance which I had experienced most vividly when gazing at the proscenium arch of an opera theatre. Returning to Venice—for, of course, I had been there before, when I sat in a gondola at the funfair—proved a moment of great poignancy. When I first stepped into the great piazza in front of San Marco on a spring afternoon, the golden sunlight slanting across the domes of the basilica, the pigeons clustering around the base of the bell-tower, the well-dressed and sophisticated people crowding the terraces of the famous cafés, I experienced the joy of one of those moments in life that we never forget. From the window of my modest room in a pensione on the Giudecca I could catch a glimpse of San Giorgio rising majestically from the lagoon. I went to a performance at La Fenice, map in one hand as I followed the twisting lanes leading to that jewelled theatre. After the performance I watched elegantly dressed Venetians boarding their waiting gondolas.

Rome enchanted me. Its layers of history piled indiscriminately on top of each other appealed to a long-dormant love of romance. I thought for the first time in years of that novel about Leonardo that had sustained me through some of my darkest childhood days. The sight of the Castel Sant' Angelo against a stormy sky, or the gloomy interior of a baroque church, smelling of mould and incense, reminded me of that night long ago when I sat in our box at the opera hypnotised by the scene-painter's attempts to reproduce these places on the stage. I fell in love with the soft round names of Roman streets, churches and palaces. Santa Maria Sopra Minerva, San Pietro in Vincoli, San Clemente (with its three levels, one a Mithraic shrine), Sant' Agnese, all the churches of Rome, the beautiful as well as the hideous, provoked emotions that I could not have experienced anywhere else. To walk down the Via Giulia, lined by mighty Renaissance palaces with laundries, motorbike repair shops and ice-cream parlours in their ground floor premises, or to wander through the narrow streets and alleys of the old ghetto near the river were sensuously romantic experiences. I was strolling through a vast and brilliant theatrical illusion where people seemed to live more intensely than I had ever thought possible.

The elegant nonchalance of Paris did not make the same impression on me as the flamboyant theatricality of Venice and Rome. But I responded to its imperial vistas, to the reminders of the *grand siècle* scattered around the Marais, to the life of the smart boulevards of the right bank and to the less stylish but equally fascinating heterodoxy of those on the left. It was in Paris, and to an extent in Italian cities, that I began to recognise images of a former life—which I had enjoyed only vicariously—that were dimly reflected by the espresso-bars of Sydney. I would sit for hours in Parisian cafés, both great establishments like the Flore and the Deux Magots and small unpretentious neighbourhood bars and brasseries, observing the public social life that Europeans, usually confined to small and inconvenient flats, lead in cafés, bars and restaurants. I realised that the people surrounding me, who talked with animation, even perhaps passion, without however losing a palpable though essentially indefinable urbanity, were more attractive, much less bizarre than the patrons of Quittner's and the Twenty-One. Was this the difference, I wondered, between Western and Eastern Europe? Was this a society which that other world, mirrored by those antipodean establishments whose patrons, lacking entirely the style and sophistication of these people, merely aped and parodied? Was I at heart a Western European, even though I was born in the despised east, and had spent more than half my life at the other end of the earth?

I could not solve these conundrums, for something had held me back from exploring again the world I had left, making me invent all sorts of excuses—it was too far, it would be too expensive, it might be a bit boring—for not going in those years at least as far as Vienna, where I could have seen at first hand some remnants of the heritage I had lost. I suspect that I avoided the east of Europe because I still carried too much of a residue of that irrational guilt I had experienced throughout those grim years in Epping, when I felt a deep shame for having been born in a place that spawned refs, balts and wogs.

Yet I also knew that I had to keep the allure of Western Europe at arm's length, that this world was not for me. No matter how beguiling I found the life of the great cities of France and Italy, I realised that by inclination and education, by the very fact of having spent so many years in Australia, my spiritual home lay, if anywhere, in England. I was also coming to understand that in England I would always be living a lie; that perhaps in Australia, precisely because I lived there day after day, year after year, I might gain greater acceptance and toleration in a society lacking deeply ingrained traditions or rituals. I realised that no matter how long I might live in England, no matter how well I might learn to mimic its ways and customs, I would remain forever the outsider, the person whose account of his origins ('I live in Australia', 'I lived in Australia for many years', 'I spent much of my childhood in Australia') would come to sound more and more shady and suspicious. And yet, several violent changes of mood suggested to me, it need not be like that. Others like me had found England a warm and welcoming society. When I tried very hard to think who they might be, I could only come up with Arthur Koestler—and he was exceptional.

These problems came to a head in the late autumn of 1962, when a great smog descended on London ahead of a winter of exceptional severity. *A Study of the Life and Works of James Shirley* was duly submitted, examined and its author was awarded the degree of Doctor of Philosophy by the University of London. I had, a month or two earlier, applied for a lectureship in Sydney. Now I was told that there would be a position falling vacant at University College, where I had done my doctoral work, which would be mine for the asking. In that sulphurous November, when I spent many hours in air-conditioned cinemas to get relief from the poisoned atmosphere, at a time when even the toothpaste had taken on the taste of pollution, I grappled with a dilemma that several of my contemporaries also had to face in those years: should I live abroad, or should I return to what I had to call, for lack of a better term, home?

Three people I had known in my student days in Sydney had to face in those years choices very similar to mine. One had no doubts at all, it seems to me, about what choice he should make. I ran into Clive James, fresh off the boat from Sydney, on the night of my *viva voce* examination in 1962. He was standing at the back of the old Sadler's Wells Theatre where the Hamburg Opera was performing *Lohengrin*. We exchanged a few words, promising to meet soon. I did not see him again after that night until some years ago when we spoke briefly at a party during one of his visits to Sydney. James obviously made the correct decision. It would have been entirely impossible in the sixties, or at any other time for that matter, to achieve in Australia a career of the kind he carved out for himself through the combination of great talent, skill and a determination to succeed. England offered him the stage on which he might exploit his considerable but perhaps unusual gifts—part intellectual, part academic, part poetic, part literary, with a large dose of the *farçeur* thrown in for good measure.

It was obvious also, during the late fifties, when I knew him well, better indeed than I knew James, that Australia would not satisfy Robert Hughes's ambitions. Almost from the first day I met him, when he fetched up at the office of the university newspaper to offer his services as a cartoonist, he spoke of the need to get away, to find some place—England? America?—where his talents might be better appreciated. We were not inclined to believe him: not because he lacked talent— on the contrary, he is one of the most talented people I have ever run across—but because so many of us entertained fantasies about how we would one day conquer the world that it was by no means unusual to meet yet another young man (ostentatiously sporting a black beret) who was about to conquer the world. Hughes, in those days, was much more sophisticated than James. Unlike the boy from Kogarah, he came from a patrician family (of somewhat reduced circumstances, it is true) which gave him the social confidence to continue in his chosen role of an *enfant terrible* after he left youth and Australia behind.

Hughes and James found a world in which they were able to grow and prosper. Both are familiar names to people throughout the English-speaking world, and beyond. They have been able to influence opinion, attitudes and ways of looking at the world in a manner that would have been impossible had they stayed at home.

And yet, is it sour grapes, I often ask myself, that makes me suspect that James had greater potential, could have achieved finer, more lasting things, could perhaps have discovered more grace and dignity than the James I see on television cracking endless series of one-liner gags, winking, even leering at his devoted studio audience (and at the global village), living to the full that carefully nurtured image of a balding larrikin in an expensive suit? Has he sold himself short by carving out a brilliant career for himself through a trick of inverse mimicry and parody, hiding his bright light under a vulgar bushel to give his British audiences the image of Australia they require, mixed with considerable intellectual dash?

In the same way, I wonder what would have become of Hughes had he not found an international stage on which to enact his ceremonies of the now ageing *enfant terrible*. Would he have become the painter he always said, in those Sydney days, he wanted to be? Should he have chosen a life of greater obscurity in Sydney or even in the bush where he might have been able to paint those canvases which, he said, were clamouring to be given life? Would that, moreover, have satisfied the need he demonstrated, from the time you first laid eyes on him, to be noticed, to be admired and, best of all perhaps, to be considered a trifle shocking? These can only remain questions. James and Hughes could not have returned to Australia; they were driven by imperatives which made no other choice possible for them.

The third of these people represents a very different phenomenon. Until the success of *The Road from Coorain*, Jill Ker Conway was not widely known outside academic circles, despite her inclusion some years ago in *Time* magazine's cover-story of eminent women. I knew her as Jill Ker. She was probably the most brilliant of my contemporaries at university, a woman of great beauty, charm and poise who carried her academic accomplishments with an easy grace. She was very good company, great fun to talk to, lively, amusing but never relaxing the elegance of personality or the intellectual rigour she has always retained. In our student days, I used to think of her as one of the lucky people. She was well-to-do, and could therefore indulge herself in those civilised pleasures of life many of us yearned for but could not afford. She had already been abroad; she was on intimate terms with people of influence we admired from afar—her teachers at university obviously held out great hope of a brilliant academic career for her. And she achieved that in America, rising not merely to the heights of her profession, but to a position of considerable influence in political and business circles as well.

When I see her nowadays, on one of her brief, often hectic visits to Sydney, I can glimpse in the confident and sophisticated woman, whose speech betrays the soft, civilised accents of Ivy League America, something of the shining person we knew at university many years ago. Instead of compromising her integrity, as a somewhat later refugee, Germaine Greer, has in her headline-grabbing outbursts of stridency, Ker Conway has grown, developed and found herself to an extent that would have been impossible in Australia—if she had not been driven out by the appalling prejudices against intellectual women among the public institutions of the day. And yet occasionally and fleetingly I catch in her something that might be regret, perhaps a moment of wistfulness. Suddenly she seems a trifle vulnerable, or lonely. I ask myself whether her life suffers from the effects of uprooting, just as my life has also suffered from the inevitable consequences of exile. The instant always passes. Jill Ker Conway, the respected historian, university administrator and public personality, pulls herself together and takes up the threads of the conversation with her customary wit and sophistication.

For these people, despite the minor disadvantages of exile that each might suffer, the decision not to return to Australia was obviously the correct choice. In Britain or the United States they had come home to their true inheritance, and there they flourished in a way that would have been impossible in their nominal homes. I do not think any of them, not even Ker Conway, will ever return to live in Australia. In my case the decision was not so simple. I lacked their confidence. But above all, at the end of 1962 when I had to choose between the prospect of a position in London and the offer of a post in Sydney, I finally chose the latter for a number of complicated reasons.

I did so partly because the uncertain and often unstable life I had led throughout my childhood and adolescence— when financial insecurity had replaced the much greater perils of war—had conferred on me what is probably an excessively pessimistic temperament. To this day I constantly expect things to go wrong—and they usually do—and I am always intent, therefore, on recognising the advantages of the bird in the hand. I was, in addition, increasingly concerned about my parents, whose business affairs had begun to turn sour, and whose cheerful letters could not disguise the worry and anguish, and, worst of all, the deteriorating personal relationship that I was to find on my return to Sydney.

But most of all, I think, I was driven to return to the place I provisionally thought of as home because deep down I knew that I could not succeed with my mimicry, my parody of an Anglo-Saxon way of life, in a world jealous of its traditions and social rituals. I realised in those last weeks I spent in London, as the great smog was replaced by a bitter blast of wind from the north, that my decision three years earlier not to accept the advice of people in Sydney, whose judgment I respected, that I should study at Oxford was probably the first warning of my reluctance to risk exposure to a tradi-tionally British academic life with its arcane rituals and ceremonies. I suspected that I would be safer in the cosmo-politan anonymity of London. Having lived in London for almost three years that suspicion was confirmed; I came to the clear realisation that I could not attempt to remake my life a second time. I could not face the prospect of being obliged once more to adopt the vigilance and desire to learn to fit in with the ways of another world that had marked my early years in Australia, even if in this second instance I would be starting from a position of considerable advantage. I accepted, therefore, the position in Sydney.

The Agent-General for New South Wales paid for a first-class berth on the *Canberra*, the newest and most glamorous of the P & O fleet, which was to sail from Southampton in the last days of 1962. The night before I left London a massive snowfall brought the city to a standstill. I managed somehow to get to Waterloo for the boat train. The station looked like a film set for the fall of Shanghai. Eventually a train was produced which crawled to Southampton preceded by a steam-locomotive spraying boiling water on the rails to unfreeze the points. I was exhausted and relieved when I was shown to my cabin, having reached Southampton many hours after the official sailing time. On the coffee table I found a large bouquet of flowers with a card reading 'Bon Voyage and Lots of Happiness to Darling Valmai from all the Girls'. The steward whisked the vase away, apologising profusely, and asked whether he should lay out my dinner jacket. I decided to take a shower in the generous bathroom attached to the cabin. The semicircular perspex shower-screen got stuck, trapping me inside the humid little cubicle. The bell was far away, out of reach near the washbasin. I remembered that my mother used to get her wedding ring off her swollen finger by rubbing it vigorously with soap. I rubbed the runners of the contraption and managed at last to escape. I went down to the dining saloon in my David Jones dinner suit.

A couple of nights later, on New Year's Eve, the Captain made a speech wishing us every success and happiness for 1963. He announced with considerable pride that his splendid crew had increased the ship's speed to such an extent that we would berth in Naples on schedule, where we would pick up those passengers who were prevented by the terrible weather from reaching Southampton by the time we had been obliged to sail. I spent a pleasant day in Naples saying goodbye to Europe, confident that I would soon be back on study leave. We sailed in the evening. The people who had missed the boat in England spoke of their relief; they were looking forward to a voyage they had thought they would have to forgo. I stayed up late into the night to catch a glimpse of Stromboli. I could see nothing; the volcano was asleep. A few hours later I was standing on deck at a lifeboat station. Clouds of acrid smoke were billowing out of the ship, bells were ringing without cease, planes of the Royal Air Force circled overhead, while I shivered in my life jacket, clutching my passport, my traveller's cheques, a carton of cigarettes and the two volumes of *A Study of the Life and Works of James Shirley*.

BETWEEN
TWO
WORLDS

Canberra. A sparkling autumn Sunday in 1991. The stifling heat of the last few days has lifted. Crystals of ice suspended high above the hills glitter in the bright sunshine. At the university a writers' festival is drawing to a close. For two days I have been watching, from the sidelines, the rituals of contemporary literary life. In the quadrangle, under deciduous trees which are just beginning to show the first signs of a response to what they have been led to believe is autumn, groups of writers, critics, publishers and hangers-on are striking deals, making or murdering reputations, or just gossiping. Soon there will be another book launch where someone will say something flattering about a mate who had probably said the same things about the launcher at a similar function not very long ago.

In the meeting rooms and lecture halls the last papers, readings and discussions are taking place. A well-dressed feminist is telling anyone who cares to hear how much she is marginalised by a patriarchal society. Yesterday a British writer got into hot water for saying that we Australians seem to have achieved a great deal in two hundred years. That provoked outrage and breast-beating protestations of guilt from people who are, almost without exception, what one may continue to call for the next week or two Anglo-Celtic—though probably some of them already know that very soon that term will also be proscribed. I do not, however, see a recognisable Koori anywhere. Many people have already left. Some are waiting anxiously for taxis to take them to the airport so that they may continue their busy lives on Monday morning. The well-known writer of thrillers has already gone, having left early in the morning to return home to feed his dogs. Those of us who remain are thinking about what we have to do next week.

A few kilometres away, on the other side of the lake, groups of people are converging on a sprawling white building (which looks from the distance like a 'Spanish' project home of generous proportions) set in the middle of a sea of tall dry grass. Though there is no other building in sight, the roadway is meticulously kerbed and guttered. There is, however, nowhere left to park. Like the other latecomers I have to drive into the waist-high grass, hoping that I will be able to drive out again. I join the people making for the building. A large red, white and green flag flutters from a mast set in the gravelled yard. Many of the people, I notice, are wearing little bows made out of plaited red, white and green silk threads. The courtyard is crowded. People are smiling, shaking hands, kissing, embracing, slapping each other on the back. A man with a clipboard is saying something to a group of attentive girls and boys in colourful costumes. The cool air is suddenly rent by the banshee whine of feedback from a loudspeaker.

Today marks Hungary's national day, commemorating the beginning of the uprising in 1848 which almost succeeded in throwing off the yoke of the hated Habsburgs. The festival atmosphere is prompted, however, by something more significant than the celebration of an unsuccessful revolution which started 143 years ago. This is the Hungarian Embassy. For the first time it has thrown its doors open to the expatriate community of Canberra and the surrounding districts in a spirit of reconciliation. These people, who left their homeland at various times in the course of the previous forty years, are no longer regarded as traitors. The hand of friendship is extended to them by the representative of the democratic new order in that faraway land, which had recently gained its freedom after almost half a century of Soviet domination.

Someone finds a place for me to sit in a row of plastic chairs placed under a colonnade, and introduces me to a couple of people while, on a small dais in the courtyard, a woman in a long black dress and sunglasses, apparently a famous Hungarian actress from New York, recites with palpitating emotions and flailing arms a turgid poem about freedom that everyone around me seems to know. How do I happen to be here? I am asked in reasonably correct English. I am spending a few days in Canberra, I explain, and have come at the invitation of one of the Embassy people. How nice, their looks seem to say; but we fall silent because an elderly man, also carrying a clipboard, now mounts the dais and embarks on an interminable account of the sufferings of the Hungarian people, and of their heroic attempts to throw off the oppressor in 1848 and 1956. He does not mention, it occurs to me, that other oppressor, whom I saw many years ago welcomed with open arms by people waving little flags with swastikas on them. A kind person offers to translate for me. No need, I smile, I can understand much of it. General surprise: how do I come to know Hungarian? I was born there, I say. And then, even before the elderly woman in the fashionable white linen suit has a chance to open her lips, I know what she is about to say: 'But you don't look Hungarian!' And indeed I do not.

In England I was not able to pass myself off as Australian in front of people who knew what Australians looked like—something like those people at the writers' festival at the other end of town who are dressed in their carefully chosen 'bush gear', worn, as everything seems to be these days, in order to make a statement. Now, among these people with high cheekbones, and the indefinable but unmistakable look of the steppes in their eyes, who have always believed that they, the Magyars, were the only true Hungarians, I seem as alien, perhaps even as much of a charlatan, as I did to those English men and women whom I told, in my innocence, that I was Australian. But the people sitting and standing around me in the brilliant sunshine, as the boys and girls in national costume begin to twirl to the accompaniment of a tape fed through an improvised public address system, betray no trace of the puzzlement those English people betrayed. They understand only too well. They look at my face, at my build and features and they know that of course I could very easily have been born in Budapest. Yet in their eyes that gives me no licence to call myself Hungarian—perhaps one or two of them might have already noticed that I had been very careful in my choice of words: 'I was born there.'

Throughout the long years of trying to come to terms with Australia, of shrugging off the isolated instances of bigotry and race-hatred I have encountered ('Fuck off you bloody wog, can't you see that's my parking place?') I had all but forgotten hatreds of another kind I had witnessed in my childhood. I now begin to search the faces of these people around me, most of them alive with emotion and patriotic pride, trying to work out how old they might be, wondering whether any of them, as very young men and women, could have spat and jeered at those lines of people, wrists tied to wrists with long strands of rope, as they were dragged off to be killed on the embankments of the Danube.

I had asked myself the same question a couple of months earlier as I sat through an interminable Christmas Day mass in a pretty Gothic church on a hill overlooking the graceful curve of the Danube that separates the two parts of Budapest. On the first Christmas Day that going to church was no longer considered an indefensible activity, I was listening to an ancient priest with amazement and distress as I began to realise that he was intoning a discredited part of the old Catholic liturgy, the prayer for the conversion of the Jews. I now understand, more fully than ever, as the folk-dancing reaches a climax of twirling and stamping, that this is not my world, not part of my heritage, just as that dead world of the espresso-bars, whose denizens would not come to a celebration like this even if they were fit enough to make the journey, had little to do with my life, with what I am or have at least become, even though I cannot discard its influence or the marks it has left on my personality.

At a convenient gap in the proceedings, I murmur my apologies in English—once again I am reluctant to speak Hungarian—extract my car from the grass, and head back across the lake to the university. The writers' festival is all but over. Only a few people are left among the long shadows of the quadrangle. The last bits of sound equipment, cartons of books and empty wine flagons are being packed away. On the way to my room, where I intend to put my feet up and watch the final episode of 'Rumpole', I stop to have a long chat with an acquaintance. We agree that the festival has been fun and proceed immediately to say how awful so-and-so's been, how we're sick to death of the way such-and-such constantly goes on about this and that, how it's a shame that some people are able to find publishers for the muck they churn out year after year, whereas others are having an uphill battle in these days of austerity, when publishers are only interested in books about pets and sex. And I realise once again that this is much more my world than anything else I've encountered in the course of the day, or, for that matter, than any country I have visited or lived in briefly in the decades since my return to Sydney on a Qantas 707 in January 1963, still shaken by the experience of fire at sea.

I may have no more than a legal right to call myself Australian, and as I look at daily life around me, I am not at all sure that I would want to identify myself entirely with the Australia in which I live. As the years go on, I find myself increasingly intolerant of the crassness and vulgarity of the urban hothouse I see each day. The packs of oversexed teenagers milling around the cinemas in George Street, the empty-headed young women in tennis dresses congregating for hours around their four-wheel drives in the carparks of suburban shopping centres as they gossip in their rising intonations, the dreadful jargon that passes for literary criticism these days, the unwillingness of contemporary undergraduates to read anything written before about 1975, the pot-bellied executive types nattering into their portable phones in restaurants and at street corners, the abysmal lack of integrity in political life, the intellectual poverty of much Australian writing—these and much, much else make me ask at times what I am doing here, whether I am living in a backward, second-class world rapidly sinking into material as well as spiritual mediocrity. But I remind myself that people like me are often prone to confuse cause and effect, shadow and substance. In the streets of London and Paris, of Munich and Vienna, I see much the same crassness, much the same vulgarity that irritates me in Sydney, though it is often in a different key in those cities, and possibly less offensive because less familiar. I wonder whether I am blaming Australia for the discontents of middle age.

I am nevertheless more Australian than anything else. This is the only society with which I am at all familiar, where I feel least alien. This is the world where I have put down roots, and a world where I have, I allow myself sometimes to think, made a small contribution. There is no other home for me. I have to come to terms with being the type of Australian I am, and I have learnt that I must no longer entertain fantasies of what I am or what I might become. I realise that the programme of assimilation I had set myself in those grim days in the Idiots' Class or among the paspalum of Epping represented an aim which could never be fully achieved. I could not remake myself, just as I could never throw off entirely my physical, emotional and spiritual affinities with the gesticulating world of the espresso-bars. And yet I have become Australianised, if it is possible to invent a word as ugly as that. The remnants of my heritage exist within a consciousness and a sensibility that were largely formed by the experience of growing up in Australia. Nothing that I could have attempted to do would have been able to achieve whatever balance there happens to be between my various cultural and spiritual selves. That balance had to emerge in the way it has, and, of course, it could just as easily have developed in an entirely different way, given other circumstances and a different temperament. My assimilation, or the extent to which I may claim to represent multiculturalism—it comes to the same thing eventually—has come about as an inevitable consequence of my personality and of the environment in which I live, but it has nevertheless emerged in a wholly haphazard manner. It could not have been otherwise.

For that reason, I view with alarm and misgivings those programmes of multiculturalism that provide a powerful preoccupation for the political and cultural life of the nation. Occasionally, I still see remnants of the few cultivated members of espresso-bar society when they meet in a suburban town hall where recitals of chamber music are given. Bent and frail, many showing recognisable signs of major surgery and courses of chemotherapy, they gossip in reedy voices with liberal use of the scatological vocabulary of their culture. There are many younger people in the audience too, some young enough to be my children. Looking at them you would think that they are ordinary middle-class citizens of Sydney, which they are in most ways. But their speech betrays something quite individual. They speak Hungarian, employing those indecent expressions that even now must not be spoken aloud in English, and using the same gestures as those elderly people, despite the fact that their years of exposure—since birth in most cases—to Australian ways should have imposed on them an entirely different pattern of behaviour. When they turn to address a remark in English, you can hear faintly but distinctly the unmistakable awkwardness with diphthongs and accentuation that distinguishes their parents' or grandparents' attempts at Australian-English.

Were these people consciously encouraged to retain what they thought was their heritage? I do not know, for since my parents' death I have drifted away entirely from that world. Whether they should be encouraged to continue in their ways is a much more pressing and difficult question. There is no reason, as far as I can see, why a genuinely free and tolerant society should not accommodate people who are different—as it must tolerate and regard as full members of the community those people who are immediately identified by their appearance as belonging to a particular ethnic type. Problems arise where these people are urged to think of themselves as different, as set apart. This seems to be the danger among those groups who are intent, on religious or social grounds, to retain certain customs that are clearly out of step with the way of life of most people in contemporary Australia.

A growing problem in universities, for instance, is the reluctance of certain Mediterranean people to allow their daughters to attend classes unchaperoned. Their solution to this problem—since most realise that institutions would not tolerate the presence of large numbers of chaperones in already overcrowded lecture rooms—is to insist that their daughters must always remain in the company of young women of their own nationality, or in many cases members of their family and immediate social circle. Their fears about their daughters' virtue are probably ill-founded. Nevertheless one would not wish to encourage them, despite the protestations of ideology, to abandon entirely social standards which have sustained their way of life for centuries. Yet to continue the practice inevitably isolates these young women from the world in which, for better or worse, they must live. The dilemma has no easy solutions; no amount of bureaucratic or ideological management or interference will make it any easier for these people to achieve a balance between their two worlds.

It is essential, nevertheless, that we should not encourage people to live in ghettoes that threaten to shut them out of those structures of society where they might flourish and prosper in a material as well as a cultural sense. Australian Catholicism has learnt the painful lesson that you must not enclose yourself behind walls of doctrine and tribal loyalties. Yet several other groups seem to be intent on committing the same errors—one might even include among these the more extreme separatist elements of the gay culture or the feminist movement. I would not want to advocate a return to those days of the late forties and the fifties when a naive notion of the possibilities of assimilation, which was merely an aspect of the larger demand for social conformity, drove people like me to attempt to jettison vital parts of our heritage. We have to be given the liberty to realise that we must, for better or worse, dwell between two worlds; and we must be allowed to work out our cultural salvation in terms of our individual, often confused, personalities, predicaments, fears and aspirations. Above all, we must realise that such a process may well take a long time, perhaps the whole of a life, to achieve.

As I am writing these words in the late autumn of 1991, I fancy that it is only very recently that I have come to anything like a clear understanding of these puzzles and predicaments. The reason for that is, of course, that after almost half a century of evasion, reluctance and perhaps even cowardice, I finally succeeded in laying to rest some noisy ghosts when I went back, briefly and provisionally, to visit the city where I was born.

My return was a reverse-image of the way I left Budapest in 1946. On a gloomy November afternoon in that year, my parents and I boarded a decrepit train, pompously entitled the Orient Express, in a soot-blackened and bomb-blasted railway station. We sat apprehensively on the worn velour seats of our compartment. The panelling above our heads still bore signs of a former world in the shape of several faded photographs, behind almost opaque panes of glass—images of the marvels of prewar Europe. As the train groaned through a desolate countryside, our anxiety increased to near-intolerable levels when we realised that we were approaching the border. Would our exit permits be honoured by the Russians? Would we be searched? Would they find the last of our gold coins in the hollowed-out heels of my mother's winter boots? After an interminable delay, the grim-faced border guards left the train. With a clang and a grating of metal we lurched forward, towards Vienna and freedom. Several hours later we were travelling in an open horse-drawn carriage down a broad street lined with the empty shells of apartment blocks and grandiose imperial palaces to our hotel in the Graben, where a small pane of glass set in the boarded-up window of our room afforded a glimpse of that once elegant thoroughfare.

A few days before Christmas in 1990, I set out from another—perhaps the same—small hotel in that street, now a pedestrian mall glittering with affluent brilliance. My elder son sat beside me in a purring Mercedes taxi as we were driven to the station along that avenue down which I had been driven, in the opposite direction, almost half a century before in a state of over-excitement because we were embarking on the great adventure that was to carry us to the other end of the world. At the well-kept, efficient station, my son and I boarded a sleek modern train, also called the Orient Express, though not that essay in nostalgic kitsch which carries the super-rich between Paris and Venice. Whereas the train my parents and I travelled on in 1946 was half-empty, the Orient Express of 1990 was filled to the brim with a noisy and excited crowd. We found our reserved seats already occupied. A few stern words in English swiftly displaced the usurpers. Meanwhile more and more people piled into the carriage. Soon the corridors were jam-packed with passengers perching on suitcases and large cardboard boxes fastened with sturdy rope.

Eventually the train moved off, half an hour late, to the relief of the generally animated and in some instances inebriated travellers. A neat, tidy Austria slid past in the gathering dusk. Darkness had fallen by the time we reached the border. Out of the window of our compartment I could see a corner of a squat utilitarian building. Through the glass panel of a doorway you could glimpse a customs official busily at work at a desk under a naked, low-wattage light bulb.

Outside, a railway worker in a shabby coat was stamping his feet in a puddle of melting snow.

The crowd fell silent. Something was in the air. It soon became obvious that the border-guards were making their way down the carriage. People began to betray the unmistakably apprehensive look of those who had lived under (or had escaped from) oppressive regimes. I noticed that they were impressed and not a little envious as we got out our Australian passports. We were the fortunate ones; we belonged to that privileged world towards which my parents and I had set out all those years ago, tense with anxiety as we sat in our compartment listening for the approach of the guards. And I, protected though I was by my magic passport, shared the tension and anxiety of my fellow-passengers, while my son sat beside me absorbed in the book he had been reading ever since darkness fell. For him this was just another frontier.

The past should not, perhaps, be revisited. Those days I spent in Budapest were among the most painful experiences of my life, for they forced me not only to remember things long forgotten, but also to recall those other days—in Hurlstone Park, in Epping and in other parts of Sydney—that were the occasion of much humiliation and shame. Walking around the decaying streets of a once graceful city, I continually thought of the dead—of all those people, my father's large family, the much smaller circle of my mother's relations, who had disappeared, vanished from the face of the earth. I recalled the days my father spent wandering those streets in 1945, when he had barely recovered from his injuries, because someone had told him that he thought he had seen my uncle, ghastly and emaciated, groping his way along one of those thoroughfares. I also remembered the terrible day when my father accepted the inevitable, that it was useless spending another day searching for a brother he would never find.

I also remembered in those streets, in gloomy cafés and

restaurants, and in the faded splendour of my hotel room where the television churned out alarming news about the war which was to break out in three weeks' time, that it was here that the seeds were sown of those black years of my parents' life in Australia, when they could not bring themselves to speak to each other, when they used me as an intermediary, and also as an emotional buffer and punching-bag.

My memories jumped years and continents. Catching sight of a group of intense and overpainted elderly ladies in a café one afternoon reminded me of a similar group in another café—in Double Bay, many years ago—who were discussing with loud exclamations of anguish and dismay the brutality of the world (this world) which they had to flee. I remembered my own sense of guilt that day, as I began to persuade myself that perhaps the vulgarity of those people was excusable in the light of their sufferings, until I realised that they were recounting the plot of *The Sound of Music*. I wondered what these ladies of 1990 were talking about. A little later that day, I recognised the baths where my mother and I had to cart bagloads of money, and still did not have enough for the price of admission. That made me recall the embarrassment of a picnic at Palm Beach on which some well-meaning acquaintances had taken us in the early years of our life in Epping. My mother was an undisguised picture of misery as she sat under the tarpaulin stretched between two cars, swatting at mosquitoes with a rolled-up newspaper in the manner we were taught to disperse the red-backs that infested our dunny. I found the pond where I used to go skating, during trips to the city made precisely for that purpose, under the eagle-eyed supervision of one or another German nanny, and the nearby restaurant where I used to be taken for a special treat. I could not, however, find many places I tried to revisit, having only confused and muddled memories of things that had been suppressed for many years.

In the life of the city I began to discern certain alarming signs that I was to see again a couple of months later in the courtyard of the Hungarian Embassy in Canberra. Magyar nationalism was visible everywhere, mixed with a totally incompatible and entirely irrelevant nostalgia for a Habsburg past. Antisemitic slogans, in a world where, surely, there were few Jews left, were daubed on walls and embankments. A statue of the Empress Elisabeth, after whom generations of Austro-Hungarian girls (including my mother) had been named, was in the process of being elaborately restored. The monument to St Stephen, king and missionary who gave my father his name, displayed once more the royal emblems of the former kingdom. It was as though the previous forty-odd years had never occurred. The wave of nostalgia and sentimentality, in a world of grim economic hardship where a couple of Australian dollars would take you in a taxi from one end of town to the other, seemed at times a distraction, at others almost an indecency. And as I walked among these people I realised that they assumed, as the people on the train assumed and as my companions at the Embassy in Canberra were to assume, that I was a foreigner. They would come up to me in the streets with offers to exchange money delivered in various languages, but never in Hungarian. In restaurants waiters would hand me, before a word had been spoken, the English or German versions of the menu. For them I obviously represented that golden world beyond the Austrian border, where elegant people strolled along well-swept boulevards, where sleek limousines deposited glamorous patrons at the vast portals of a huge opera house, where everyone could afford to buy genuine Levis and wear Reeboks to their hearts' content.

I had nothing in common with this world, I came to realise as the initial impact of return began to wear off. This was not my life; it had almost no bearing on what I was or felt myself to be. I began to be acutely aware of the advantages of my real life. Sydney, with its sprawling suburbs, its harsh, all-revealing light, seemed a blessed place compared with the murk and grime of this depressing city. I glanced up at a first-floor window; someone was leaning out, staring at the tramlines on the street below. I thought of Sydney—how if

I lean out of our bedroom window I can just catch sight of a square of blue water with a headland above it that reveals at night those twinkling streetlights my parents and I saw as the *Marine Phoenix* sailed towards the Heads. In this, my home town, I did not dare to board the clattering trams for fear they would bear me off to places unknown, from which I would have trouble getting back to my hotel. The language that people spoke all around me, though comprehensible, seemed strange and foreign. Their ways were alien and a trifle menacing. I did not know how to deal with the many people importuning me to buy this or that. I got confused about the elaborate rituals governing café-life: who served, whom to pay, how to tip, and when to leave. I realised that I desperately wanted to go home.

In the train to Vienna, after it had pulled out of the seething railway station, where you felt you had to hang on to your wallet for dear life, I fell into conversation with an elderly couple, vaguely reminiscent of the patrons of Sydney's espresso-bars of former years. They had just been to Budapest for the umpteenth time to visit relatives for Christmas. They'd had an absolutely wonderful time. I mentioned something about the grime and the filth, the air of depression that hung over the city. They hadn't noticed. Mind you they didn't go out much, there were so many relatives to see. And the food! They wouldn't want to eat another thing until they got back to Toronto for New Year. People back home sure knew how to be hospitable, especially now that life was so much easier. I smiled and changed the subject; quite obviously, we had been visiting different worlds.

For a few days after I got back to Sydney I looked around me with changed eyes. This was home; this was where I belonged. The old life was no longer meaningful to me except as a source of anecdotes, to which middle-aged people are frequently and at times tediously addicted. But those few days in Budapest had, it seems to me, loosened a spring, or perhaps lifted a lid, allowing long-suppressed memories to escape. They were, in a way, my own madeleine, dipped in this instance into a polluted and noisome river. And as I slipped back into the familiar routines of Sydney life, taking up the threads that I had dropped a couple of months before when I flew out of Mascot in a screaming Jumbo, convinced, as I usually am, that we would crash at any moment, I found that in an intangible and not entirely clear way the present and the past, those seemingly absolutely contradictory experiences and ways of life, were parts of a larger whole. I cannot explain what that whole might be—it is probably indistinguishable from the process of living. But I came to learn something that 'normal' people, those whose lives have not suffered the sharp cleavage mine seems to have suffered, have always known: that the past may yield sense only in terms of the present, and that the present is inevitably conditioned by the past. To remove either of these—as I tried to suppress my past during the years of my adolescence, and as the more extreme theories of multiculturalism urge people to ignore the realities of the present—is capable of leading to a serious and damaging spiritual imbalance.

I cannot pretend that that realisation has made me any happier, any more content with my lot, or given me a clearer idea of what I am. As the days and weeks wore on after my return, I felt again the old doubts and uncertainties returning. Had it all been a mistake? What would life have been like if my parents hadn't bundled me out of Budapest on that foggy November day in 1946, with a scarf wrapped around my head because I was still sick with mumps? Should I have waited for that position at University College London, after all? My moods changed as rapidly as they always have. Among my family and friends, people who have given shape, meaning and purpose to my life—which seems otherwise something of a bad joke—I feel contentment and peace. At other times, as I watch the increasingly mindless rituals of many aspects of academic life, or as I listen to the strident, often ill-informed and alarmingly unintelligent punditry that pours out of the radio and television hour after hour, I think that back there, in that possibly imaginary Europe of my fantasies, things might be better ordained—that in an older and more mellow society life might be less fraught with the irritations and vulgarities of life in the raw. Then I hear a snippet of news about the ugly racial tensions that are once more surfacing in those nations which have recently won their independence from Soviet control, and I begin to wonder whether that unhappy continent isn't about to start again down the road towards the hatred and enmity that tore it apart half a century ago, provoking people like my parents, and millions of others, to flee to the farthest corner of the globe.

And, as always, I experience the old fears and alarms. A screaming siren in a distant street, heard on a still summer night, leaves me edgy and apprehensive. I begin to wonder, with that clarity of vision which is ours in the dead of night, whether, as the economic difficulties of contemporary Australia bring out of the cupboard ugly hatreds that had been hidden for a long time, I will also have to experience what members of my family, and millions like them, had to endure. I think back on the world into which I was born—my great-grandfather the supervisor of milk in his proud uniform, the elderly ladies chattering in my grandmother's living-room as the great tile stove sent out waves of comforting heat on a dark winter afternoon, my mother peering with short-sighted eyes through a pair of gilt opera-glasses. They too felt safe. They too imagined that being citizens of a country where their families had lived for generations would protect them against atrocities like those their ancestors had to suffer. They were, after all, respectable Hungarians and Austrians of the twentieth century, paying their taxes, observing the customs of a country in which they felt entirely at home. That reassuring stove, which the maid dutifully stoked up each morning and evening, was as close as all of them thought they would get to a fiery furnace.

Will I also find, I ask myself as the siren recedes into the night, and as I think of those slogans I see daubed on walls and fences ('Australia for Australians', 'Stop Migration Now') all over the city, that my father's naturalisation certificate, on which I am included almost as an afterthought, will prove to be as worthless as the documents which promised my parents, and their parents before them, safety and security in their homeland? Will my sons have to appeal one day to the fact that their mother was a fourth-generation Australian in order to obtain permission to remain here? These are probably the fantasies of an overwrought imagination; but on those still nights they are, nevertheless, menacing realities which I cannot entirely banish.

I shall probably experience for the rest of my life these doubts and alarms. This is, in all likelihood, the yoke of exile. There is nothing, in the final count, to be done about it except to understand the predicament and to come to terms with it to the best of one's ability. There are no solutions, no reassuring slogans to assuage doubts, alarms and perplexities. People like me will probably search and seek, wonder and question, and suffer from irrational fears to the ends of our lives. We must acknowledge that we belong nowhere, that our sense of dislocation is more radical and more disturbing than the characteristic alienation most people experience from time to time in their familiar world. We have no place we may call home truly and unconditionally, for we are always aware that we were born elsewhere, and that our lives are governed by the consequences of a choice we exercised, or of a decision that had been exercised on our behalf.

We are essentially rootless. Try as hard as we might, we cannot feel at one with the world in which we live—the only world we know, the only world, indeed, prepared to accept us, even if only provisionally, and on rare occasions with bad grace. For many of us the place where we were born has become more alien and much more perplexing than anything we encounter in our daily existence in the world we must think of as home. We come to understand, therefore, that we belong nowhere—yet sometimes we still dream of an existence where we may avoid the confusions of lives like ours, which seem more and more to resemble the nightmare of that ingenious puzzle, a loop without an inside or an outside.

BLESSED CITY
Letters to Thomas Riddell 1943
GWEN HARWOOD

At the beginning of 1943, the year in which these letters were written, Gwen Foster was twenty-two and living with her family in Brisbane. During the week she worked as a clerk at the War Damage Commission, and on Sundays she was the organist at All Saints' Church.

Gwen Foster was to become the acclaimed poet Gwen Harwood. The letters, written to her friend, Lieutenant Thomas (Tony) Riddell, are a wonderfully entertaining account of her family, of daily life in wartime Brisbane, of her reading and love of music and of her detested job at the War Damage Commission, a kind of Circumlocution Office weighed down by its own files and tied up in red tape. Lively, amusing and sometimes moving, these letters provide a fascinating early portrait of one of Australia's most important writers.

'Wartime letters to a serviceman from a witty, affectionate young musician and nascent poet with a sharp eye and a sharp tongue are, to Harwood's generation and to later ones, an amazing gift.'
KERRYN GOLDSWORTHY, *AUSTRALIAN BOOK REVIEW*

'Sensual, satirical and often wickedly funny, *Blessed City* is more than an original work, it is an illumination.'
THE JUDGES, THE *AGE* BOOK OF THE YEAR AWARD, 1990